1986

Duquesne Studies

LANGUAGE AND LITERATURE SERIES

VOLUME FOUR

GENERAL EDITOR

Foster Provost, *Department of English, Duquesne University*

Faire Bitts

Piero di Cosimo, THE FOREST FIRE (detail)
Courtesy Ashmolean Museum

Faire Bitts

Sir Philip Sidney
and
Renaissance Political Theory

Martin N. Raitiere

Duquesne University Press
Pittsburgh

Published by:
Duquesne University Prss
600 Forbes Avenue
Pittsburgh, PA 15282.

Distributed by:
Humanities Press
Atlantic Highlands New Jersey 07716.

First Edition

Library of Congress Cataloging in Publication Data

Raitiere, Martin N., 1948-
  Faire bitts.

  (Duquesne studies. Language and literature series; v. 4)
  Includes bibliographical references and index.
  1. Sidney Philip, Sir, 1554-1586—Political and social views. 2. Sidney, Philip, Sir, 1554-1586. Arcadia. 3. Languet, Hubert, 1518-1581. 4. Politics and literature. I. Title. II. Series.
  PR2343.R38   1983   821'.4   83-11705
  ISBN 0-8207-0162-9

For Betsy, Sasha, and Holden

Contents

Preface

1   Introduction   3
2   Amphialus' Rebellion: The Arcadian
    Use of History   19
3   War in Sparta   39
4   Give Us a King: Philisides' Fable I   57
5   Man Was Not Man: Philisides' Fable II   79
6   Conclusion   103

Appendix A: Hubert Languet's Authorship of the
    Vindiciae contra tyrannos   113
Appendix B: Fulke Greville on "Ister Banke"   143

Index   151

Preface

THIS IS A STUDY OF A POEM in Sir Philip Sidney's *Arcadia*, and, through that poem, of Sidney's political orientation. Perhaps I should explain why Sidney's politics and why that one poem.

We need a serious study of Sidney's political views. Although studies on Sidney have flourished during the past couple of decades, his political views have more often been taken for granted than studied. What William Godshalk suggested in 1972 remains true today: "We still need a . . . comprehensive synthesis which attempts to place Sidney's theoretical and political work in context with his fiction and poetry."[1] While not attempting such a synthesis myself, I have chosen to provide the groundwork for it by engaging what seems to me to be the most problematic political statement in *Arcadia*—the text where the reader remains most in need of help and the text that serves as a key to Sidney's political orientation generally.

Sidney's politics have been misconstrued because we have put undue emphasis on some obvious biographical facts. Being a hero does not always serve a man's cause. Fairly continuously since his death in the Low Countries, we have known what we wanted out of Sidney: we have cast him as the *beau idéal* of English Protestant chivalry. This preconception may have kept us from evaluating correctly what Sidney wrote.

The tendency to construe the struggle of the Low Countries

---

[1]William Godshalk, "Recent Studies in Sidney," *ELR* 2 (1972), 156.

ix

against Spain as a type of the struggle for liberty against oppression, and the Dutch republic thereby formed as one of the first modern constitutional states, did not end with the historian J. L. Motley. Given that it was a Spanish bullet that shattered Sidney's thigh, he must be a frank partisan of modern constitutionalism:

> Then Phil spread out his map—the map of Europe. "Here, my friend, is the setting for our Protestant League—the League that will make us a united world.... The tyranny of spain will be over at last." ... If he saw Protestantism as progressive, it was because he felt that it had been allowed to flourish only in those countries in which the back of economic feudalism had been broken. He foresaw a great faith rising from the spirit of the common people; and from this faith, built on its most solid rock, a new type of civilization in which all men's rights would be on equal footing. As the feudal lord believed in the divine right of kings, so Phil believed in the divine right of the people. Perhaps in his own lifetime the scepter might pass from noble to commoner.... And all over Europe the torch of William of Orange had set bonfires of liberty alight.[2]

It is true that this purple passage comes from a novelized biography. However it would not be difficult to show that (with certain exceptions to be duly noted) much serious criticism argues for, or rather assumes, the same position: views Sidney as vibrating in sympathy with a pan-European Protestant resistance.

I differ with most previous critics in two ways. I am more than happy to acknowledge the overwhelming biographical evidence that connects Sidney solidly to the continental architects of modern constitutionalism. If anything, I believe that Sidney knew the Protestant resistance literature more circumstantially than anyone has suggested, and indeed commented on it in his *Arcadia*. On the other hand, I argue that Sidney commented on it in order to reject it.

This doesn't mean that Sidney didn't take seriously his allies in the Protestant resistance. He took them very seriously indeed. One doesn't bother to refute someone whose views do not touch one closely. Sidney bothered because he was concerned. Thus I stress both aspects—the poet's circumstantial involvement with the resist-

---

[2]Dorothy Norris Foote, *The Constant Star* (New York: Charles Scribner's Sons, 1959), pp. 55, 59.

ance literature no less than the fact that he comments on this literature in order to reject it.

Although it is evident elsewhere, Sidney's concern with the Protestant resistance crystallizes in one poem above all. I argue that this
poem constitutes a specific comment on that most notorious of Protestant works, the *Vindiciae contra tyrannos,* a work written by one of
Sidney's intimates in the Protestant vanguard. Accordingly, of my
four central chapters, the first two may be viewed as a preliminary
orientation to this poem, while the last two engage the poem in
detail. Either we take the time to construe this poem properly, or we
miss Sidney's central political statement. There is no getting at Sidney apart from his politics, and I am afraid there is no getting at
Sidney's politics apart from this poem. I should add that I believe
this poem a great one, deserving of the kind of attention that this
study attempts.

This brings me to the issue of proof. To mention that notorious,
pseudonymously published *Vindiciae* is to raise the vexed question of
its authorship. It seems to me that we can with a fair degree of
certainty resolve this question and that such a resolution throws an
interesting light on Sidney's poem. A positivistically inclined scholar
may say that a reasonable case is not enough. While it is true that no
one has left us with a signed confession admitting to the authorship
of this work, it strikes me as a hopeless exercise in Pyrrhonism to wait
for the discovery of such a document before moving to certain
commonsense conclusions. For the convenience of the reader, I
have placed the material regarding the *Vindiciae* in Appendix A.

Does the following discussion bear any relation to contemporary
political debate? We tend to conceive of political rights as being
private property. This conception goes back to Locke and, before
him, to Sidney's Protestant allies. Sidney's understanding of politics
and of the state directly opposes such a view. Since it may not be
clear to all of us how political rights could be anything other than
private property, any articulate challenge to that conception may
promote an examination of our own political assumptions.

On the other hand, we have to be careful in translating from
Sidney's time and terms into ours. I'm not sure that any of our
favorite political catchwords and oppositions—e.g., "conservative"
versus "radical"—have immediate sixteenth century equivalents. Although I argue that Sidney rejected the doctrine of aboriginal polit-

ical rights, this is not necessarily to cast him as an unadulterated "conservative"—it was precisely the resistance theorists' claim to be "conserving" some antecedent order that drew Sidney's skepticism. I am not saying that the transition between Sidney's time and our own cannot be made, but that it has to be made with a certain tact. Kings (and resistance to them) may not be what they used to be, but insofar as he deals with the perennial theme of freedom Sidney can still speak to us.

* * *

For teaching me much of what I know about Renaissance literature in general, I am grateful to Edward W. Tayler, P. Jeffrey Ford, and the late William Nelson. I would also like to thank Annabel Patterson, David Bevington, and Foster Provost for constructive criticisms of the manuscript. The following argument on Sidney remains, of course, my responsibility. Chapter Two has appeared previously in *Journal of Medieval and Renaissance Studies* and Appendix A in *Il Pensiero Politico;* I am grateful for permission to reprint.

Faire Bitts

CHAPTER ONE

Introduction

There want not some subtle stratagems of importance, and some
politic secrets of privity, in the [*New Arcadia*]
— Gabriel Harvey, *Pierces Superogation*

[1]

THERE IS AMPLE EVIDENCE for Philip Sidney's interest in such
French thinkers as François Hotman, Philippe de Mornay, and
Hubert Languet. Thus in 1959 J. H. M. Salmon was able to claim that
Sidney served as a crucial link tying Protestant French politics to
Elizabethan England.[1] What is the significance of those thinkers who
constitute Sidney's French connection?

A number of Sidney's Protestant allies interest the modern student of political theory because they comprise a group of thinkers
who have come to be called "monarchomachs." This term, a
neologism from Greek meaning "king-fighter," was confected by
William Barclay, a Scottish royalist who published a refutation of
their theories in 1600.[2] Although Barclay was certainly correct to
view these thinkers as forming a coherent school, and correct to
discern in this school the potential for an antipathy to kingship, the
term he coined is somewhat misleading since the Protestants he had
in mind did not oppose kingship as such but rather absolutism.
Nevertheless the term "monarchomach" has stuck, and it is not
without a certain aptness, for these writers did articulate a clear

---

[1]J. H. M. Salmon, "Some Personal Links between English Statesmen and French
Theorists." Appendix B of *The French Religious Wars in English Political Thought* (Oxford: Clarendon Press, 1959).
[2]William Barclay, *De regno et regali potestate: adversus Buchananum, Brutum,
Boucherium, et reliquos monarchomachos* (1600).

3

theory of resistance, one that influenced later and more uncompromising attitudes.

The three principal monarchomach works, then, are: François Hotman's *Francogallia* (1573); Theodore Beza's *Du droit des magistrats* (1574); and the *Vindiciae contra tyrannos*, published in 1579 under the pseudonym "Stephanus Junius Brutus." The Scottish writer George Buchanan, who has some close connections to the French scene as well as to Sidney, works the same mine of ideas in his *De jure regni apud Scotos*, also published in 1579.

These works have both a narrowly polemical and a more broadly theoretical interest, although the occasional polemic is skilfully submerged in the theoretical discussion. Most immediately the French works are concerned to attack the Valois monarchy of the 1570s, that is, Catherine de'Medici and her sons Charles IX (1560-1574) and Henry III (1574-1589), whom they represent as degenerate Italianate tyrants. Although the "trauma theory" according to which this literature sprang into existence as a response to the St. Bartholomew's Massacre of August 1572 has certain shortcomings, we have nothing to gain from denying all sorts of connections between the most ostensibly disinterested monarchomach literature and the day-to-day course of practical politics in the 1570s.[3] For the monarchomachs clearly wanted the Valois out and their own Protestant people in.

On the theoretical plane, one may briefly indicate their significance as follows. In the words of one modern scholar, the monarchomach works "constitute a clear and definite transition from medieval to modern constitutional ideas."[4] To the notion of the supremacy of law, rooted in earlier political tradition, these works join two additional concepts: (a) the idea of a sovereign community from which all authority derives; (b) regular institutional controls, by the people or their representatives, of derived authority. The frank and confident articulation of these two ideas distinguishes the monarchomach works from earlier ones, e.g., Marsilius of Padua's *Defensor Pacis*, in which similar ideas appear in less systematic form.

Forty years ago, a historian of ideas traced the American Declara-

---

[3]Ralph Giesey has demonstrated that the earliest monarchomach work was not drafted in response to St. Bartholomew: "When and Why Hotman Wrote the *Francogallia,*" *BHR* 29 (1967), 581–611.

[4]Julian H. Franklin (trans. and ed.), *Constitutionalism and Resistance in the Sixteenth Century* (New York: Pegasus, 1969), p. 11.

tion of Independence back to the *Vindiciae contra tyrannos*. This may have been simplistic since it has recently been suggested that we should locate Jefferson's ideas in a context other than the individualistic one that Becker proposed.[5] But broadly speaking we may say that the modern tradition of popular sovereignty and the supremacy of representative bodies originates in the monarchomachs.

Each of the three key works differs somewhat in its conception of the institutional controls on royal power. For Hotman in the *Francogallia*, it is the Estates General that has full responsibility for supervising the king. For Beza in the *Droit des magistrats*, such responsibility is shared between the Estates and the so-called inferior magistrates, meaning, loosely, any territorial prince, town magistrate, or other official beneath the king in status but otherwise legally constituted and recognized. For Junius Brutus in the *Vindiciae*, such responsibility falls more or less exclusively to the magistrates.

These differences reflect changes in the political situation through the 1570s during which time the works become increasingly radical. In 1572, writing much of his tract before St. Bartholomew, Hotman is not so much interested in recasting the political structure as in reminding the Estates of what he conceives to be their ideal supervisory role. By 1574, writing in the wake of St. Bartholomew, Beza is interested less in the ideal functioning of the state than in the means of resistance to corrupt authority. By 1576 (the probable date of composition of the *Vindiciae*, published three years later), Junius Brutus drafts nothing short of an invitation to rebel. His *Vindiciae* is the most impassioned of the three French works. Junius Brutus invites and encourages a military struggle against the Valois monarchy, a struggle that depends for primary leadership on the great territorial nobles and only secondarily on the Estates, whom the Protestants have little reason to regard as an agency of radical change.

Certain other differences in tone and idiom mark the three works. Hotman's *Francogallia* is explicitly a humanist's description of past French history and only implicitly a political message for the present. Hotman argues that the Frankish monarchy in Gaul re-

---

[5]Cf. Carl Becker, *The Declaration of Independence* (New York: Alfred A. Knopf, 1942), pp. 33–34; Becker's conclusions are questioned by Garry Wills, *Inventing America: Jefferson's Declaration of Independence* (Garden City: Doubleday, 1978).

sulted not from conquest but rather from a free and voluntary asso-
ciation of Franks and Gauls who jointly elected a single ruler. In the
beginning, therefore, the French kings were the creatures of the
community. At some point, however, this relation was reversed since
presently the community subserves the king. For all its scrupulous
descriptivism, no one was likely to miss the central polemical point of
the *Francogallia:* let us go back to the early days, recover the antique
constitution, and make our rulers accountable to us. In case anyone
did miss it, someone writing under the name of "Eusebius Philadel-
phus Cosmopolite" popularized Hotman's argument in 1574 in a
dialogue called *Reveille-Matin* which explicitly spelled out the
polemical purpose of such "historical" investigations. The two later
monarchomach works do not, at any rate, disguise their polemical
intentions beneath such antiquarianism.

These are, however, differences of emphasis or idiom rather than
of substance. The three works may justly be considered to comprise
a common statement. All three insist that sovereignty derives from
the community and must operate under certain institutional controls. The three works draw on many of the same sources: Aristotle
and other classical theorists of the rule of law, Roman civil law, and
(for Beza and Junius Brutus) a common fund of scriptural examples. Further, many links exist between the three authors. Beza was
in touch with Hotman while writing the *Droit des magistrats* and
showed him the manuscript before publication,[6] and Junius Brutus
in turn drew heavily on Beza's work and, as we shall see, had many
personal connections with the anti-Valois opposition. It is clear that
all three French works, along with Buchanan's *De jure regni,* emerge
from a fairly coherent and cohesive pan-European network of Protestant writers and thinkers.

Lastly, any discussion of the monarchomachs encounters the
vexed question of the identity of "Stephanus Junius Brutus." Who
wrote the most radical of the three French works? It seems to me
that we possess all the evidence we need to answer this question: the
author was Hubert Languet. As I don't wish to encumber my central
thesis with this question, I refer the interested reader to Appendix
A, where I present all the evidence and draw the commonsense
conclusion. As I noted earlier, I have not discovered Languet's

---

[6]Cf. Theodore Beza, *Du droit des magistrats*, ed. Robert M. Kingdon (Geneva: Droz,
1970), p. xxvii.

signed confession. And no *one* of my articles of evidence decides the issue. But taken together they amount to what I think is a convincing case. From this point on, I assume the conclusion drawn and defended in Appendix A — Hubert Languet's authorship of the *Vindiciae contra tyrannos*.

Hubert Languet is the Frenchman whom every biographer of Philip Sidney since Thomas Zouch invariably identifies as the poet's guide and mentor. That the most radical work of the French wars of religion should have been authored by the man regularly identified, even by their contemporaries, as Sidney's tutor, raises a number of interesting questions. Principally: do Languet's political ideas leave any kind of an imprint on Sidney's fiction, the *Arcadia*, the first version of which was written but one year after the publication of Languet's work in 1579? Did Sidney accept Languet's political program? I believe that we can answer both of these questions satisfactorily.

[2]

Any student of Sidney knows that the poet's life is closely interwoven with the cause of English and continental Protestantism.

Sidney's father, Sir Henry Sidney, had orchestrated English aid to the Huguenots in the early years of the French wars.[7] Sidney's mother, Mary Dudley, was the sister of Robert Dudley, Earl of Leicester, for many years the leader of Protestant activism in England. While Philip seems to have been recognized as an engaging and witty young man by most of the individuals who met him, let us admit that it was principally as Leicester's friend, nephew, and heir apparent that he was courted by leading Protestants, both English and continental. It was no mean connection, and Sidney, who considered it his "chiefest honor . . . to be a Dudlei,"[8] knew it.

Hindsight tells us that the cause of what has often been referred to as the Sidney, or Leicester, or Walsingham circle had fizzled by 1588, by which time all three of these men were dead. But through the 1570s and early 1580s the Leicester bloc represented a primary activist power in England, one of which the latitudinarian Elizabeth

---

[7]Cf. Salmon, p. 184.

[8]A. Feuillerat (ed.), *Prose Works of Sir Philip Sidney* (Cambridge: University Press, 1962), 3:66. Further references to these *Prose Works* will be incorporated into the text.

was often wary. This bloc stood, among other things, for a franker engagement in the affairs of England's continental allies than Elizabeth desired. This is not to say that Sidney agreed with all of Leicester's and Walsingham's goals: I shall argue that on certain important matters he did not. But whether Sidney liked it or not, he was certainly viewed by his contemporaries in terms of his attachment to Leicester. It seems clear that Sidney's connection to the activist party has a good deal to do with his chronic inability to find favor in the eyes of Elizabeth herself.[9] This circumstance helped to keep Sidney's power rather more potential than actual.

As an eighteen-year-old, Sidney witnessed one of the crucial political events of the 1570s. In July 1572 he went to Paris as part of the English contingent attending the nuptials of Henry of Navarre and Margaret of Valois. Several days after the August wedding, Catherine de'Medici was dissuaded from her ordinary policy of balancing peacefully the Guise faction against the Protestants. Thus on St. Bartholomew's Day the Guise faction, with the complicity of Charles IX and his mother and the aid of the Paris underground, slaughtered some two to three thousand members of the opposition including its leaders Condé and Coligny. Legend has it that Charles IX himself, who had a reputation as a great hunter, picked off Huguenots from his palace window with his crossbow. While this was going on Sidney and the rest of the English contingent took refuge at the English ambassador's residence. James Osborn has tentatively identified as Sidney a young English gentleman whom the Duc de Nevers escorted the next morning to view some Huguenot corpses.[10] We need not accept this to suppose that Sidney must have been profoundly impressed by St. Bartholomew. When revising his *Arcadia* some twelve years later, he added a wicked queen-mother figure who is generally believed to owe something to Catherine de'Medici.

Sidney stayed on the continent for some three years (1572-1575). During this time he was introduced to many of the leading Protestants who, now irremediably polarized against the Valois, were regrouping and redefining their objectives. It is unclear when he first met François Hotman, author of the *Francogallia*. Writing to Hot-

---

[9]Cf. James Osborn, *Young Philip Sidney* (New Haven: Yale University Press, 1972), p. 497.
[10]Ibid., pp. 69-71.

man's son Jean in 1580, he spoke of his "amour de cette eccellent personnage vostre pere" (3:134) and subsequently placed Jean as secretary to Leicester in the Netherlands campaign.[11] Philippe de Mornay he met in 1572, and by 1577, when Mornay visited England, he and Sidney were on good terms. Mornay asked Sidney to be the godfather of his child born in England in 1577.[12] Sidney later began an English translation of one of Mornay's principal works, the *Vérité de la religion chrestienne,* published in French in 1581, although most of the published English translation is by Arthur Golding.

Sidney knew many other key Protestants. As James Phillips shows, George Buchanan, author of the monarchomach *De jure regni apud Scotos,* was in effect sponsored by the Leicester bloc (which Phillips terms the "Sidney circle," perhaps misidentifying its true locus of power or assuming more than is strictly fair about Sidney's adhesion to his uncle's policies).[13] Sidney met Henri Estienne in Heidelberg in 1573 and later received the dedication of two of his works; Estienne's involvement in the production of Languet's *Vindiciae contra tyrannos* is discussed in Appendix A.[14] In the Low Countries, William of Orange regarded Sidney with enough favor to consider him seriously as a brother-in-law, and Louise de Coligny later remembered him warmly.[15] This list of connections to continental Protestants could be extended considerably.

[3]

The most crucial of Sidney's activist connections was obviously that to Hubert Languet, one of the most militant Protestants of the 1570s. Languet had been a disciple of Melanchthon, whose scrupulous blend of rationalist political doctrine with Biblical example leaves its mark on the *Vindiciae* (for this and all other matters relating to the *Vindiciae,* see Appendix A). As early as 1568 he wrote for

---

[11]Cf. Malcolm Wallace, *The Life of Sir Philip Sidney* (1915; reprinted, New York: Octagon Books, 1967), p. 260.

[12]Cf. Philippe de Mornay, *Mémoires et correspondance* (Paris, 1824), 1:117, 119.

[13]James Phillips, "George Buchanan and the Sidney Circle," *HLQ* 12 (1948–49), 23–55.

[14]Estienne dedicated to Sidney an edition of the Greek New Testament (1576) and an edition of Herodian (1581).

[15]Osborn, p. 491.

William of Orange a *Justification* of the Low Countries against Spain.
For most of the 1570s Languet was stationed in Vienna in the service
of Augustus, Elector of Saxony. During the winter of 1574-1575,
while at Michael Lingelsheim's house in Vienna along with Henri
Estienne and (coincidentally) Sidney, he first thought of writing
what was to become the *Vindiciae contra tyrannos*. He composed this
work during 1576, completing it by January 1, 1577, on which date
Estienne added the Preface. Although Languet expected to publish
the work in 1577, changing political circumstances discouraged him.
It was not until 1579 that Languet, by now in the service of William of
Orange, was persuaded to publish his tract as a justification of the
Low Countries revolt. In 1580 Languet published a second edition
of this work and had a hand in another Orange manifesto, the
Apology against Philip II. Languet died in September 1581, and allies
including Walsingham and Beza mourned him as a crucial figure in
the activist cause.

Languet met Sidney in Paris in 1572 and guided him on his continental tour. He and Sidney soon developed a genuine friendship.
Sidney had a reunion with Languet in Germany in 1577, when the
older man was deliberating whether to publish the recently completed *Vindiciae,* and saw him again in England in 1579. He and
Languet exchanged letters regularly until the latter's death. Languet's letters to Sidney, published posthumously in 1633 as *Epistolae
politicae et historicae,* give a circumstantial picture of European political affairs in the 1570s.

The terms of this friendship may partially have been dictated by
the age difference: when they met Sidney was 18; Languet, 56.
Languet persisted in playing a kind of Polonius to the young man,
doling out advice on matters personal and political. From such evidence the poet's biographers have invariably inferred that Languet
was Sidney's mentor. Certainly this is how Languet saw himself, and
this may be how interested contemporaries saw the relationship. In
1579 Daniel Rogers—with, be it noted, Languet at his side—
addressed an elegy to Sidney in which he claimed that Languet was
"the tutor who determined your judgment."[16] This does not mean
that Sidney saw himself in these terms, however. He surely had a
good deal of personal feeling for Languet, even stating in 1575 that

---

[16]For the text of Rogers' elegy, see J. A. van Dorsten, *Poets, Patrons, and Professors*
(London: Oxford University Press, 1962), pp. 175-179. The passage in question, as
trans. p. 65.

Languet was as a father to him (3:102). But personal friendship does not necessarily imply agreement on ideological issues.

Sidney more than once made light of Languet's admonitions to him. Languet had little in the way of flexibility and wit, whereas Sidney's wit left nothing untouched, not even the holy cause of Protestantism. If we accept the suggestion that the figure of Geryon in *Arcadia* derives in part from Languet, then we have the poet poking gentle fun at a counsellor whose advice verges on the tendentious and stuffy.[17] One of the older biographers, uncharacteristically free of sentimentality, has this evaluation of the tutor and the friendship:

> It is odd that Sidney put up with Languet's letters; their gush and piety are sickening enough today. . . . Difficult, indeed, is it to picture a high-spirited boy receiving his lugubrious and sermonising epistles with even a show of patience. . . . [Languet] was a man who made wisdom rather irritating. He was, in a word, a prig. . . . His attacks on Philip's supposed idleness are morbidly ridiculous.[18]

Whether Sidney in fact "put up with" Languet's admonitions is a question for which the rest of this study provides an answer.

So much for Sidney's personal ties to the Protestant activists. What we want to know is what the poet thought of their ideas, and to answer this question we must turn from the external evidence to Sidney's works themselves, principally the *Arcadia*.

[4]

The reader who comes to Sidney's *Arcadia* from his biography may be in for a surprise. For the fiction's general political orientation seems quite antipathetic to that of the constitutionalists who figure so prominently in the poet's life. The plot involves, more than anything else, the actions of kings. From the first page of the first version—the so-called *Old Arcadia*—the plot centers on Basilius, king of Arcadia, demonstrating the mischance that results from his acting or rather not acting as a king must. We hear mostly about

---

[17]Ephim Fogel, "The Personal References in the Fiction and Poetry of Sir Philip Sidney" (Ph.D. dissertation, Ohio State University, 1958), pp. 235–240. Fogel argues for Geron as a combination of Languet and Edward Dyer.

[18]Percy Addleshaw, *Sir Philip Sidney* (1909; reprinted, Port Washington, New York: Kennikat Press, 1970), pp. 289, 291, 289.

Basilius and his family, and almost but not quite nothing about politics other than royalist—and we hear this through 400-some pages of the *Old Arcadia* plus another 500-some of the *New Arcadia*. The basic mainspring of the plot—by not acting firmly, a king precipitates a political crisis—is the oldest one in the Elizabethan book, and should remind us far more of *Gorboduc, The Laws of Ecclesiastical Polity*, and *King Lear* than of the *Droit des magistrats* or the *Vindiciae*. Where the whole design of the constitutionalist works of the 1570s is to draw attention away from the personality of the monarch, to erect a mechanism ensuring that his or her personality never impinge directly on his *office*, Sidney's fiction reverses these priorities, making politics a function of the king's private economy and will. This is not to say that a normative element doesn't enter but rather that such an element originates with the king himself and not outside of him in some established constitutional machine. You can read through all—well, almost all—of *Arcadia* without finding any trace of those constitutional agencies that the monarchomachs insist should intervene in the king's will. No ephors, estate, or parliament step in when Basilius miscalculates. Nor does Sidney ever seem to suggest —unless the reader plead specially with a vengeance—that such agencies should intervene. Whatever connection Sidney's fiction has to the constitutionalist ideas of his French connection, they are certainly not very obvious ones. It is impossible to deny that the work's orientation is overwhelmingly royalist—simply counting pages would prove this.

How then did the problem that suggested the present study arise in the first place—the assumption that Sidney's politics are of the king-fighting species (or, as the romancer put it, that "Phil believed in the divine right of the people")?

I can think of two answers to this question. First, we all enjoy the biographical details (if we can get them, and it so happens that with Sidney we can get a good many of them) of a poet's life, and wish not unjustly to integrate his work with those details. We thus find it easy to believe that Sidney might have sympathized with the ideas of his French friends and allow this belief to substitute for the business of reading his works.

Or if we do read Sidney, we find that his work, if sparing of reference to the constitutionalists, is not devoid of them. One text in *Arcadia* explicitly mentions Hubert Languet, the greatest luminary of the Protestant resistance, and in a context that seems to indicate that the poet is paying tribute to Languet as well as to his ideas. I am referring to the political fable that occurs in the Third Eclogues of *Old Arcadia*, a fable recited by a fictional character named Philisides, generally (with what justice we shall see) considered Sidney's self-portrait. Before recounting his curious fable, Philisides (Sidney?) devotes three stanzas to a characterization of "old Languet," whom he identifies as his tutor and the source of the fable or "songe":

> The songe I sange old Languet had me taught,
> Languet, the shepheard best swift *Ister* knewe,
> For clerkly reed, and hating what is naught,
> For faithfull hart, cleane hands, and mouth as true:
> With his sweet skill my skillesse youth he drewe,
>   To have a feeling tast of him that sitts
>   Beyond the heaven, far more beyond your witts.
>
> He said, the Musique best thilke powers pleasd
> Was jumpe concorde betweene our wit and will:
> Where highest notes to godlines are raisd,
> And lowest sinke not downe to jote of ill:
> With old true tales he woont mine eares to fill,
>   How sheepheards did of yore, how now they thrive,
>   Spoiling their flock, or while twixt them they strive.
>
> He liked me, but pitied lustfull youth:
> His good strong staffe my slippry yeares upbore:
> He still hop'd well, because I loved truth;
> Till forste to parte, with harte and eyes even sore,
> To worthy Coredens he gave me ore.
>   But thus in oke's true shade recounted he
>   Which now in night's deepe shade sheep heard of me.[19]

I take these lines to be indisputably accurate, and Philisides to coincide with the poet, in one respect. They reflect biographical fact insofar as "old Languet" really did "fill [Sidney's] eares" with "old true tales" treating of the manner in which "shepherds" minister to their "flocks" (or, to unravel the pastoral metaphor, the manner in which rulers minister to their communities). For Languet shared

---

[19]Throughout this study the text of this poem as of all others by Sidney shall be taken from William A. Ringler, Jr. (ed.), *The Poems of Sir Philip Sidney* (Oxford: Clarendon Press, 1962), pp. 98–103. There is a substantially identical text in Jean Robertson (ed.), *The Countess of Pembroke's Arcadia (The Old Arcadia)* (Oxford: Clarendon Press, 1973).

with Sidney the *Vindiciae contra tyrannos* itself, a work that the poet
saw in manuscript a full two years before it was published. But
whether Sidney agreed with Languet's *Vindiciae* is another question
entirely. It is my argument that he did not, and that his demurral
from Languet's doctrine is revealed and justified in the very fable
that he ascribes to Languet.

My procedure is to compare the fictional fable with Languet's
extrafictional views. By mentioning Languet as its author, and by
alluding to his views within the fable proper, Sidney clearly wished
us to engage in such an act of comparison. When we do so we find
that the fable, so far from corroborating the position of its putative
source, in fact discredits it. I suggest that the political fable (sometimes called the "Ister banke" eclogue after the first line, "As I my
little flocke on Ister banke"), so far from being a transcription of
Languet's teaching, relates disjunctively to it and functions as a
critique of the monarchomachs.

Incidentally, such an ironic mechanism as this view implies—one
of the poet's *personae* contradicting his avowed cause—is nothing
new to Sidney scholars. Students long ago ceased to read the poet's
sonnet sequence, *Astrophil and Stella,* as biographical confession and
now distinguish as a matter of course the "speaker" of the sonnets
from Sidney himself. When we read the political fable with the same
kind of discriminating attention that the *Astrophil and Stella* poems
regularly receive, I think we'll have little difficulty seeing that Sidney
himself sympathizes no more with Philisides and "old Languet" than
with star-struck, maundering Astrophil.

[5]

If the first reason for the assumption that the poet is kin to his
constitutionalist friends reflects principally on us, the second reflects on Sidney. For he is not entirely innocent of the difficulties
surrounding our assessment of his political sympathies. Although
much of Arcadian politics seems to me to represent no special critical puzzle, it is true that the fable in question is not without ambiguity at certain points. No text is more problematic than "Ister
banke"; nowhere else in the entire fiction is the reader more in need
of help than here.

Sidney may be indirect and Aesopic here in part for a prudential reason. He is alluding to (if only to refute) some fairly radical political views held by a personal friend. In 1580 no more than half a dozen people in all of Europe knew that Languet was responsible for the already notorious *Vindiciae*. Although he needed to deal with the issues raised by Languet's treatise, Sidney surely did not wish to compromise his friend by explicitly identifying him as the author of the *Vindiciae* in a work that would circulate publicly (though to a fairly limited extent, its author apparently never intending *Arcadia* to be set up in print).

Yet I am inclined to minimize this motive. Sidney's text is problematic because he wanted it to be, not because it had to be. I think Sidney wished his reader to experience a certain amount of difficulty with his text. This is not to say that I accept a model of infinite interpretability according to which Sidney's real meaning keeps one step ahead of our constructions. I think the text means one thing, not many—yet previous scholarship if nothing else suggests we experience a certain recalcitrance in grasping that thing. Such recalcitrance, I would argue, is an organic part of the text's meaning and not a mere obstacle to be brushed aside. The recalcitrance we experience in dealing with the text is an esthetic corollary of the difficulty we should feel in accepting its conclusion, which, as we shall see, is not entirely a happy one.

One way of minimizing the difficulties presented by "Ister banke"—and they are finite—is to establish the proper context for our encounter with it. Thus the following two chapters, which prepare for the fable by discussing a couple of other hard spots. The episodes I have chosen to deal with in these chapters have generated some scholarly noise: we have no consensus on the import of Amphialus' rebellion in the *New Arcadia,* nor on the Laconian wars in *New Arcadia.* What is true of the fable is true of these texts as well, that Sidney programmed the noise right into them. Yet they are not as complex as the fable and serve as good training tools for it in two ways: they introduce us to some characteristic Sidnean maneuvers while at the same time they testify to Sidney's reasoned antipathy to the monarchomachs. In Chapter Two I corroborate the view, not original with me, that Amphialus' rebellion functions as a critique of one of the keystones of monarchomach thought—the doctrine of the "inferior magistrate" as a legitimate revolutionary sponsor. Chapter Three deals with Sidney's critique of a commonplace—the myth of Sparta as an ideal state—which we encounter not only in

Languet's *Vindiciae* but indeed throughout the liberal political tradition from Polybius to Jean-Jacques Rousseau. The reader who learns, in these two chapters, how Sidney is fencing with doctrine derived either from the monarchomachs or from the liberal political tradition generally, will not be surprised by the conclusion I draw through Chapters Four and Five, which deal with Philisides' fable.[20]

[6]

Apart from specific differences in political attitude, another issue distinguishes Sidney from the monarchomachs. This is the simple fact that he wrote a fiction. Between the utilitarianism of the Protestant resistance literature and *Arcadia* looms a gap that is not merely generic. Either you work for the cause or you dawdle—and writing fiction is clearly dawdling. Such at least was Languet's point of view. So far as I am aware, Languet knew nothing of Sidney's fiction. If he had, he would no doubt have considered it a waste of time. Languet often warned Sidney not to acquire learning that he could not quickly translate into action. Latin, for example, should be encouraged because it was good for diplomatic correspondence; but Greek was useless and should not.[21] Languet would wish impatiently to know what immediate political goal would be subserved by writing a fiction. None, of course; whatever "effects" the *Arcadia* would have would be fairly indirect. We can read Sidney's great essay in literary criticism, the *Apology for Poetry,* as a critique of the simple exemplaristic model according to which a fiction immediately and unambiguously compels the reader's will in a certain direction. Poems—Sidney's word for fictions—don't work that way.[22] By the

---

[20]I do not address the question as to whether the *New Arcadia* differs in political scope and attitude from the *Old Arcadia* because it seems to me that in this respect the similarities far outweigh the differences and that they can be discussed interchangeably without doing any violence to the poet. In regard to politics, the revision differs from the original chiefly in degree of explicitness. Thus we shall consider Sidney's texts not in the order of composition but rather according to their ease of access, with the most obvious claiming first call. References to *Arcadia* indicate both versions indifferently; the *Old* or *New* are specified as necessary.

[21]Cf. Languet to Sidney, Jan. 20, 1574. Languet's letters to Sidney, originally published as *Epistolae politicae et historicae scriptae quondam ad illustr. Phillip. Sydnaeum* (Frankfurt, 1633), shall be identified by date only.

[22]See my essay, "The Unity of Sidney's *Apology for Poetry,*" *Studies in English Literature* 21 (1981) 37–57.

fact of its existence alone, *Arcadia*, an involved, curious, and learned poem, rebukes the functionalist, puritanical, and action-oriented mentality of Languet and his cohorts. You will not find a trace of wit (not to speak of the obliquities of fiction) in the monarchomachs.

This is not, however, to represent Sidney's *Arcadia* as the mere obverse of practical and forensic reality, as an indulgence in what the poet himself in the *Apology* calls the golden world. Sidney's dismissal of his own fiction as a"toyfull book" (3:132) is a Renaissance conventionalism, and it would be critical suicide to take it seriously. The poet does not simply retreat before Languet's use-oriented exhortations but comments actively on them through the medium of his fiction. Having momentarily distinguished the poet from the writers of political treatises, we shall now return both parties to common ground. As we explore this ground, however, the reader should bear in mind that, from the Calvinist perspective of the monarchomachs, no act of Sidney's was more egregious than his decision to commit a fiction.

CHAPTER TWO

Amphialus' Rebellion:

The Arcadian Use of History

L'histoire est un mauvais roman—Diderot

[1]

IN WHAT IS PERHAPS THE CENTRAL POLITICAL EVENT of *New Arcadia*, Queen Cecropia and her son Amphialius contrive a rebellion against King Basilius of Arcadia. It has been noticed that Amphialus justifies his rebellion against his legitimate sovereign in monarchomach terms. Thus he casts Basilius as a monarch who by virtue of his defective rule may lawfully be replaced, and himself as a duly constituted "subaltern magistrate" legitimately entitled to lead the rebellion and engineer the replacement.

While this episode clearly demonstrates Sidney's familiarity with the monarchomach program including the "subaltern magistrate" theory of rebellion, scholars seem not to have reached any consensus regarding the author's own attitude toward this doctrine. Apparently impressed by the circumstantial nature of his allusions to the king-fighters, they have often supposed that familiarity argues sympathy.[1] Yet Irving Ribner many years ago cautioned that for all his knowledge of monarchomach doctrine Sidney's text suggests an attitude other than sympathetic.[2] Similarly, Richard McCoy's interesting recent study, *Sir Philip Sidney: Rebellion in Arcadia* (1979),

---

[1]W. D. Briggs, "Political Ideas in Sidney's *Arcadia*," *SP* 28 (1931), 137–61; W. D. Briggs, "Sidney's Political Ideas," *SP* 29 (1932), 534–542; Martin Bergbusch, "Political Thought and Conduct in Sidney's *Arcadia*," Ph.D. dissertation, Cornell University, 1971, pp. 80–87, 135–82; Martin Bergbusch, "Rebellion in the *New Arcadia*," *PQ* 53 (1974), 29–49.

[2]Irving Ribner, "Sir Philip Sidney on Civil Insurrection," *JHI* 13 (1952), 257–265.

emphasizes the poet's real doubts before the category of rebellion, though it should be noted that his psychologizing approach forbids him from venturing judgment on Sidney's attitude to the monarchomach documents proper.[3]

The task of the present chapter will be twofold. First, I shall vindicate the notion that Sidney's familiarity with the subaltern magistrate theory does not add up to sympathy since the poet displays the theory only to condemn it as an invitation to wholesale political unrest. Second, I shall suggest that Sidney drew inspiration from the same historical revolt that the Huguenot publicists themselves had sought to legitimize, fashioning this material, however, so as to come to a conclusion precisely contradicting that of the monarchomachs. Sidney's episode thus functions as a species of counterexemplum to Languet's *Vindiciae* and similar works: sharing common matter, the poet and the king-fighters disagree only in their construction of this matter.

The Amphialus episode of *New Arcadia* (1584) constitutes Sidney's most explicit and easily available essay on monarchomach doctrine. The so-called *Old Arcadia* (1580) does not touch on the theory of the subaltern magistrate, although we shall see that its "Ister banke" eclogue submits another aspect of monarchomach ideology to a canny allegorical critique. That the later version should make explicit what the earlier one had been content to leave Aesopic need not surprise us. In 1580 the monarchomach design was still very much up in the air, and Languet was anxious to recruit Sidney for the cause. By 1584 things were different. First, Languet, the most belligerent of the king-fighters, was gone. Second, in 1584 the entire complexion of European politics changed with the death of François duc d'Anjou. That the legitimate heir to the French throne was now a Protestant (Henry of Navarre) rendered the monarchomach arguments suddenly obsolete. An era of a certain kind of political thought, one that had begun in 1573 with Hotman's *Francogallia*, was over. This kind of political idiom had, at the moment of its ending, acquired enough definition for Sidney to write its epitaph in *New Arcadia*. Though he felt and transmitted the charm of the monarchomach argument, he judged its logic to be specious. However sententious in the abstract, Sidney suggested, this argument lends

---

[3]Richard McCoy, *Sir Philip Sidney: Rebellion in Arcadia* (New Brunswick: Rutgers University Press, 1979).

itself in actual practice to disruption of the social fabric far exceeding that which serves as pretext to rebellion. Sidney's rebelling "subaltern magistrate" uses monarchomach theory simply to further his own self-serving purposes. But he seduces only those of his countrymen anxious to convert public unrest into private gain and at last, in the classic pattern whereby evil "eats up itself," repudiates the terms of his rebellion and destroys its principal inspiration.

[2]

On the eve of his revolt against his sovereign and uncle, Basilius of Arcadia, Amphialus publishes a "justification" of his action. I quote at length the key passage, Sidney's detailed description of this document:

But because [Amphialus] knewe, how violently rumors doo blow the sails of popular judgements, & how few there be, that can discerne betweene trueth and truthlikenes, betweene showes and substance; he caused a justification of this his action to be written, whereof were sowed abroad many copies, which with some glosses of probabilitie, might hide indeede the foulenes of his treason; and from true common-places, fetch down most false applications. For, beginning how much the duetie which is owed to the countrie, goes beyond all other dueties, since in it selfe it conteines them all, and that for the respect thereof, not onely all tender respects of kindred, or whatsoever other friendshippes, are to be laide aside, but that even long-helde opinions (rather builded upon a secreate of goevernement, then any ground of truthe) are to be forsaken. He fell by degrees to shew, that since the ende whereto any thing is directed, is ever to be of more noble reckning, then the thing thereto directed: that therefore, the weal-publicke was more to be regarded, then any person or magistrate that thereunto was ordeined. The feeling consideration whereof, had moved him (though as nere of kinne to Basilius as could be, yet) to set principally before his eyes, the good estate of so many thousands, over whom Basilius raigned: rather then so to hoodwinke himselfe with affection, as to suffer the realme to runne to manifest ruine. *The care whereof, did kindly appertaine to those, who being subalterne magistrates and officers of the crowne, were to be employed as from the Prince, so for the people;* and of all other, especiallie himselfe, who being descended of the Royall race, and next heire male, Nature had no sooner opened his eyes, but that the soyle where-upon they did looke, was to looke for at his hands a continuall carefulnes: which

as from his childhood he had ever caried; so now finding that his
uncle had not only given over all care of government, but had put it
into the hands of Philanax, (a man neither in birth comparable to
many, nor for his corrupt, prowde, and partiall dealing, liked of
any) but beside, had set his daughters (in whom the whole estate, as
next heires thereunto, had no lesse interest then himselfe) in so
unfit & il-guarded a place, as it was not only dangerous for their
persons, but (if they should be conveied to any forraine country) to
the whole common-wealth pernicious: that therefore he had
brought them into this strong castle of his, which way, if it might
seem strange, they were to consider, that new necessities require
new remedies: but there they should be served & honored as belonged to their greatness, until by the general assembly of the
estates, it should be determined how they should to their best (both
publique, and private) advantage be matched; vowing all faith &
duty both to the father & children, never by him to be violated. But
if in the meane time, before the estates could be assembled, he
were assailed, he would then for his own defence take arms: desir-
ing all, that either tendred the dangerous case of their country, or
in their harts loved justice, to defend him in this his just action. And
if the Prince should commaund them otherwise, yet to know, that
therein he was no more to be obeied, then if he should call for
poison to hurt himself withall: since all that was done, was done for
his service, howsoever he might (seduced by Philanax) interprete
of it: he protesting, that what soever he should doo for his owne
defence, should be against Philanax, & no way against Basilius
(1:371-73).

As Briggs and others have noticed, this "justification" epitomizes
monarchomach doctrine. Thus Amphialus' characterization of
"officers of the crown" as "from the Prince, so for the people" depends on the familiar monarchomach distinction between those
magistrates who function as servants of the king (*regis officarii,
officiers du roi*) and those who function as servants of the kingdom
(*regni officarii, officiers de la couronne*, "officers of the crown").[4] Similarly, his identification of such officers as "subaltern magistrates"
betrays the use of a key technical term. The Huguenot theorists
warn repeatedly that private individuals have no right to take arms
against a tyrant, and regularly repudiate any popular or democratic

---

[4]For this distinction, cf. Hubert Languet, *A Defence of Liberty Against Tyrants*, a trans.
of the *Vindiciae contra tyrannos*, introd. H. L. Laski (1924; reprinted, Gloucester, Mass.:
Peter Smith, 1963), pp. 126–127, 135; also Theodore Beza, *Du droit des magistrats*, ed.
Robert M. Kingdon (Geneva: Droz, 1971), p. 18.

sentiment. Rebellion must seek sponsorship in a previously constituted authority, of which the principal form, at least for Languet's
Vindiciae, is the "subaltern or inferior magistrate." While not original
with the monarchomachs, the subaltern magistrate theory of rebellion reached its greatest development with them in the 1570s.[5]

Despite these undeniable allusions to the king-fighters, it seems
clear that Sidney condemns Amphialus' revolt. Within the rebellion
as such, he portrays Amphialus as self-serving, opportunistic, and
flagrantly false to his word. For even while vowing otherwise, Amphialus systematically violates "all faith & duty both to the father &
children" (1:372), placing the king's daughters, prisoners in his castle, in peril of their virtue and lives and doing all he can to separate
Basilius from his throne. He plans the revolt by manipulating the
individual "humors" of each group of prospective allies, tendering
to each the appropriate hope: "To his friends, friendlines; to the
ambitious, great expectations; to the displeased, revenge; to the
greedie, spoyle: wrapping their hopes with such cunning, as they
rather seemed given over unto them as partakers: then promises
sprung of necessitie" (1:371). Further, the narrator frankly names
Amphialus' action—"painted" though it may be "with rhetorical
colours" (1:373)—treason (1:371). Similarly, the narrator represents
the logic of Amphialus' "justification" as specious; from "true
common-places" this document contrives to "fetch down most false
applications"; these succeed only because its publisher realizes "how
few there be, that can discern between trueth and truthlikenes, between showes and substance" (1:371). Indeed, in due time a wiser
Amphialus himself comes to repent "the mishappes of his youth, the
evils he had been cause of, his rebelling with shame" (1:451) and
berates himself for having borne arms against his rightful prince
(1:493). Finally—as the episode slides into farce and as the rebels
self-destruct in the classic manner—while intending to kill himself
in the presence of his mother, the primary inspiration of his revolt,
Amphialus inadvertently causes her to tumble from a parapet to her
death (1:492). Thus the reader who fails to distinguish the unregenerate Amphialus' "false applications" from the "true common-
places" of which they represent a perversion recapitulates the error

---

[5]Cf. Languet, Question Three passim; also Beza, pp. 18ff. See also Richard R.
Benert, "Inferior Magistrates in Sixteenth Century Political and Legal Thought"
(Ph.D. dissertation, University of Minnesota, 1967).

of those "popular judgements" (1:371) for whom the rebel manages grateful contempt.

The central "true common-place" of Amphialus' justification is simply that of most western political thought since Aristotle, namely, the view that the political ideal is the rule of law. Amphialus follows the monarchomachs in dangling before the discontented a slicked-down version of this theme. Thus he exploits a distinction between obedience to the "weal-publicke" and that to "any person or magistrate . . . thereunto ordeined." Obey laws, not people: "The duetie which is owed to the countrie, goes beyond all other dueties" (1:371). Such a rigorous opposition between obedience to country and obedience to personal authority is characteristic of the monarchomachs rather than of more conciliatory thinkers. Michael Walzer has described the absolute impersonality of the Huguenot concept of authority, which supercedes older feudal notions of obedience to the ruler's person.[6] But no political design can absolve itself entirely of a personal element. Although to modern ears the appeal to "the duetie which is owed to the countrie" may have a fatally obvious logic about it, few sixteenth century thinkers apart from the monarchomachs were prepared to accept such an abstract concept of duty in place of the older, personally oriented one. Fewer still were prepared, granting such an acceptance, to claim that in the event the ruler does *not* respect the good of the commonwealth he should instantly be replaced. John Calvin, who was imbued with the rationalist and classicist political ideals and who thereby prepared for the Calvinist monarchomachs, is enthusiastic for the rule of law: "C'est une chose désirable . . . que les loix dominent."[7] But generally Calvin distances and contains the ideal, the normative vision, within the traditional exhortation to Christian resignation.[8] Amphialus follows the monarchomachs—and in so doing slips from the hoariest of western "true common-places" to a "false application" thereof— when he deduces from the simple postulate of a normative vision of law that the ruler who even once takes his eye off that norm is ripe for replacement. It is true that Basilius can be a poor ruler, at times

---

[6]Michael Walzer, *The Revolution of the Saints* (New York: Atheneum, 1973), pp. 68–92.

[7]John Calvin, "Sermon sur la Deutéronome," in *Corpus reformatorum* (1863–1900) 55: 459.

[8]I except the notorious penultimate paragraph of the *Institutes*, which makes an uncharacteristically radical suggestion.

even incompetent—indeed this is what starts the entire romance. It is true that his misjudgments or hesitations have severe consequences—indeed much of *Arcadia* constitutes an often hilarious catalog of these consequences. It is not therefore true that his nephew Amphialus should be allowed to chastize and replace him.

The rebellion episode is represented as Cecropia and Amphialus' wilful appropriation for their own selfish ends of the resistance rhetoric of the 1570s. Sidney wants to show how easily such rhetoric lends itself to dubious purposes. For "popular judgements" could and did forget the distinction between the "trueth" of the rule of law and the "truthlikenes" of rebellion and tyrannicide. Since there will always be a Cecropia or Amphialus around to take advantage of such rhetoric, let not the occasion for its deployment arise in the first place; let the king keep his house in order. This is the reading of Fulke Greville, Sidney's friend, first biographer, and editor of *New Arcadia*. According to him, one of the principal lessons of Sidney's work is that

> When sovereign Princes, to play with their own visions, will put off public action, which is the splendor of Majestie, and unactively charge the managing of their greatest affaires upon the second-hand faith, and diligence of Deputies [as Basilius does at the beginning of Arcadia when he elects to go on vacation] . . . even then they bring themselves and their Estates in a cloud of contempt, and under it both encourage, and shaddow *the conspiracies of ambitious subalternes to their false endes,* I mean the ruin of States and Princes.[9]

Greville's "conspiracies of ambitious subalternes" evidently refers to Amphialus' rebellion against Basilius. Had Basilius not "put off public action, which is the splendor of Majestie," thereby bringing himself "in a cloud of contempt," his subaltern would not have had the wherewithal to revolt. The normative political element, then, is charged to the person of the king rather than, as in the monarchomachs, to a constitutional agency outside the king. Sidney has no more sympathy for Amphialus *qua* rebellious "subaltern magistrate" than he does for the "many-headed multitude" of the Phagonians whose rebellion the narrator of *Old Arcadia* dismisses with such contempt (4:120ff).

[9]Fulke Greville, *Life of Sir Philip Sidney* (Oxford: Clarendon Press, 1907), pp. 11–12.

[3]

While I have clarified the narrator's judgment, I have been unable
to attend to some significant aspects of Amphialus' "justification" as
well as the steps whereby Sidney was persuaded of that judgment. In
order to do so, let us observe that Sidney did not cut the Amphialus
episode out of whole cloth. He drew inspiration, I believe, from a
specific rebellion that the monarchomachs themselves had sought to
legitimize in the 1570s, reserving the poet's and moralist's right to
modify the "bare *was*" of history by way of elaborating a satisfactory
exemplum—one, that is to say, precisely contradicting what the
king-fighters and particularly his late friend Languet had made of it.
Thus we may gain some insight into Sidney's intention and method
by observing the transformation into fictional incident from historical accident.

That accident was the attempt by François d'Anjou et d'Alençon,
some nine years before Sidney composed *New Arcadia*, to seize the
French throne. Not content with being (from 1574 to 1584) next-in-
line to the throne occupied by his older brother Henry III, this
mercurial Valois prince sought to make himself attractive to any and
all dissident groups including the radical Calvinists; thus he farmed
himself out to the monarchomachs as a "subaltern magistrate"
legitimately entitled to lead a revolt against Henry III. In the crucial
event of the fifth civil war (1574-1576), Anjou led a coalition of
so-called "Malcontents" and radical Calvinists in just such an armed
revolt against Henry. As recent scholarship has shown, two of the
principal monarchomach works provided ideological cover for this
revolt. Beza wrote the *Droit des magistrats* (1574) principally as
a justification, and with the blessing, of Anjou's ally Condé. This
Frenchman spent the mid-1570s shopping for international aid
against Henry III and in the crucial action of December 1575 was
responsible (along with John Casimir of the Palatinate) for leading
8,000 German mercenaries over the Rhine to rendezvous with
Anjou and march on Paris.[10] Further, we now know that Languet
composed the *Vindiciae* in 1575-1576 as a justification and ration-
alization of the Anjou-led revolt (see Appendix A). Ever the most
conservative of revolutionaries, Languet insisted not only that the

---

[10]For Beza and Condé, see E. Droz, "Fausses adresses typographiques," *BHR* 23
(1961), 380–385, 572–574.

sponsor of rebellion be a duly constituted subaltern but also that he be in the Valois line of succession if not in fact the younger brother of the king[11] — a proposal that may strike us as absurdly counter-productive until we recognize the role of Anjou in his design. In fact the *Vindiciae* comprises but one of a cluster of documents that, accepting the postulate of an alliance between Anjou's Malcontents and the Huguenots (formalized in 1574), looks to Anjou as the engine of France's reformation.[12]

Several reasons compel me to discern in the fictional rebellion echoes of Anjou's. First and least significant, we know that for another action of Amphialus, Sidney drew inspiration from Anjou's life. Greenlaw long ago pointed out the resemblance of the mother-and-son teams Cecropia-Amphialus and Catherine de'Medici-Anjou. He observed that Cecropia's scheme to obtain Basilius' throne by marrying Amphialus to one of his two daughters derives from Catherine de'Medici's scheme to obtain the English throne by marrying Anjou to Elizabeth.[13] Sidney may thus have taken the liberty of conflating into related schemes against a single throne two distinct acts of Anjou — his notorious attempt to wed Elizabeth of England (which had Catherine's blessing) and his equally notorious revolt against Henry of France (which as it happens did not). By adducing the 1575-1576 revolt as a model for Amphialus', I am simply generalizing the extent of his debt to the French prince.

Second, at the core of Amphialus' "justification" is not a single argument but a dual one, the halves of which coexist uneasily. Amphialus claims that the responsibility to revolt falls not only to the subaltern magistrates in general but "especiallie [to] himselfe, who

[11]Languet, pp. 121, 123–124.

[12]These documents include *Discours merveilleux de la royne Catherine de Medicis* (1574); *Lunettes de christal de roche par lesquelles on voit clairment le chemin tenu pour subjuger la France a mesme obeissance que la Turquie* (1576); *La France-Turquie, c'est-a-dire conseils et moyens tenu par les ennemis de la couronne de France pour reduire le royaume en tel etat que la tyrannie turquesque* (1576); *Epistre aux delicats et flateurs machiavelistes, qui ne peuvent trouver bonne la prinse des armes contre la tyrannie violente des perturbateurs de l'Estat du royaume de France* (1575); *Resolution claire et facile sur la question tant de fois faite de la prise des armes* (1575); *Discours sur les moyens de bien gouverner et maintenir en paix un royaume, contre N. Machiavel Florentin* (1576). For an account of the Anjou-led rebellion, cf. Francis De Crue, *Le Parti des Politiques au lendemain de la Saint-Barthélemy* (Paris, 1892). While François did not acquire the title of Anjou until 1576, I shall call him by this title throughout for the sake of consistency.

[13]Edwin Greenlaw, "The Captivity Episode in Sidney's *Arcadia*," in *Manly Anniversary Studies in Language and Literature* (Chicago: University of Chicago Press, 1923).

being descended of the Royall race, and next heir male, Nature had
no sooner opened his eyes, but that the soyle where-upon they
did looke, was to looke for at his hands a continuall carefulnes"
(1:372)—that is, Amphialus claims his being heir to the throne gives
him first crack at the "tyrant." If this is sophistical (one might object
that a subaltern with no family connections might prove a more
responsible engine of reformation than one related to the offending
ruler), if this betrays an uneasy alliance between the rationalistic
argument in favor of constitutional supervision by a class of "subaltern magistrates" and the merely historical insistence on family continuity, then precisely the same confusion of motives obtains in the
case of that cluster of documents published in defense of Anjou's
revolt including the *Vindiciae*. J. W. Allen, for example, found that
treatise's insistence on keeping the crown in the Valois line quite
puzzling; it was only when more recent scholarship perceived Languet's relation to the Anjou revolt that the puzzle was solved.[14] Thus
the same appropriation of disinterested resistance theory by a
highly interested prince of the blood royal featured in Amphialus'
revolt had some years earlier been illustrated to Sidney by Anjou's
revolt and its attendant polemic.

Third, Amphialus' "justification" bears a resemblance to a
number of manifestoes justifying a call to arms that issue from the
French wars of religion but perhaps to none so closely as a *Protestation* that Anjou himself published in 1575 on the eve of his revolt.[15]
On several points the correspondence between this and the fictional
document is noteworthy. Both constitute theoretical justifications of
rebellion against a sovereign monarch by a young, ambitious, and
not unattractive heir to the throne. Both, perhaps inevitably, use the
same general argument: that a kingdom subsists only by respect for
law, and that should the monarch be derelict in his maintenance of
the law, then it falls to the proper authorities to chastize him. To this
argument from the rule of law, both documents append that from
heredity, for the author in each case is not just any rebel but next
heir male to the throne. Both documents contrive not to impugn the
king directly: in each case blame devolves on those in an advisory

[14]Cf. J. W. Allen, *A History of Political Thought in the Sixteenth Century* (1928; reprinted, New York: Barnes & Noble, 1960), pp. 320–331; also Salvo Mastellone,
"Aspetti del'antimachiavellismo in Francia: Gentillet e Languet," *Pensiero Politico* 2
(1969), 376–415, especially p. 410.

[15]*Protestation de monseigneur filz & frere de roy, duc d'Alençon* (s.l., 1575) (unpaginated).

capacity to the king (Basilius' advisor Philanax, Henry III's Italian-ate entourage). In both cases the upstarts piously absolve themselves of any design on the king's person. Both documents mask the de-fender's aggressive action by terming it a largely defensive and pro-tective one and only incidentally offensive—an equivocation that neither author bothers to maintain for long, for both documents end with a disingenuously worded call to arms. Both documents call for a general assembly of the estates by way of redressing the king-dom (the fictional one gives the estates the added task of marrying off Basilius' daughters). Both documents are sown abroad as well as at home.[16] Both documents are immediately preceded by the rebel's dispatching of private letters to any possibly sympathetic nobles.[17] Sidney's description of the public response to Amphialus' mani-festo—it prevails with some "of more quick then sound conceipte" to join him and breeds in others "a coolenesse, to deal violently against him, and a false-minded neutralitie to expect the issue" (1:373)— amounts to an accurate description of the manner in which Europe responded to Anjou's in 1575. I think it is safe to say that however modified by fictional exigencies, the first inspiration of Amphialus' manifesto was the cognate document published by François d'An-jou.[18]

Fourth and lastly, the narrator's censure, within the fiction, of Anphialus' revolt accords with Philip Sidney's extrafictional censure of Anjou's revolt and with his general disapproval of the Valois prince. Anjou had invited Sidney himself to join in his rebellion against Henry III. This invitation, dating from April 1576 or just before the Paix de Monsieur whereby Anjou settled with Henry, coincides with a general effort on Anjou's part about this time to ingratiate himself with Protestant notables including Hotman and

[16]While Amphialus' manifesto is "sowed abroad" (1:371), Anjou's was quickly trans-lated into English as *Protestation of the most high & mightie Prince Frauncis, both Sonne and Brother of King* . . . (s.l., 1575) and published again in Geneva in 1576, for which edition see n. 24 infra.

[17]For Anjou's letters to the French nobility, cf. Kervyn de Lettenhove, *Les Huguenots et les gueux* (Brussels, 1883–1885), vol. III, p. 547. Compare Amphialus' dispatching of "privat letters to al those principall Lords and gentlemen of the country, whom he thought ether alliance or friendship to himselfe might drawe" (1:371).

[18]I make this claim at the risk of becoming mired in *Quellenforschungen*. One may prefer to claim that Amphialus' "justification" should be referred to a genre, that of the self-serving manifesto of the French civil wars (various examples of which could be adduced) rather than to Anjou's document alone. While Anjou's manifesto seems to be the most appropriate, I am only too happy to grant that our focus should ultimately be less on the poet's model(s) than on his modifications thereof.

Mornay.[19] Sidney refused the invitation.[20] Further, students of Sidney are familiar with his famous 1579 letter to Elizabeth excoriating her suitor Anjou. To illustrate the French prince's self-serving nature, Sidney reminded Elizabeth of Anjou's "inconstant attempts against his brother" (3:54), by which he meant principally the 1575-1576 revolt. Sidney also criticized Anjou for "thrusting him self into the low countrey matters" (3:54), indicating Anjou's negotiating with William of Orange for the sovereignty of Flanders and Brabant. Although Languet—who in 1580 secretly played a key role in securing Anjou's sovereignty of the Low Countries provinces and whose *Vindiciae* had a vested interest in Anjou—repeatedly suggested that Sidney would have little to gain from attacking the Valois prince and in fact urged his young friend to cross the channel and join Anjou's force in the Low Countries, Sidney remained adamant in his opposition.[21]

Over the nine years that intervene between Anjou's revolt against Henry III and Sidney's recasting of it in *New Arcadia*, many of Anjou's original allies among the Calvinists came to share Sidney's disapproval. He lost most of these allies in 1577 by deserting to his brother's court and then, as head of the royal armies, slaughtering Huguenots in two encounters, a fact of which Sidney later reminded Elizabeth (3:52). His subsequent accord with Orange, nominally in the service of the Protestants, met with widespread skepticism; apart

---

[19]For Anjou's offer to Hotman, cf. Beatrice Reynolds, *Proponents of Limited Monarchy in Sixteenth Century France: François Hotman and Jean Bodin* (1931; reprinted, New York: AMS Press, 1968), p. 87; for his relations with Mornay, cf. *Mémoires et correspondance de Duplessis-Mornay* (Paris, 1824-25) 2:79-80.

[20]See James Osborn, *Young Philip Sidney* (New Haven: Yale University Press, 1972), pp. 421-422, 434.

[21]On January 30, 1580, Languet wrote to Sidney: "The party and influence of Anjou is on the increase here [in the Low Countries], and if you should annoy him by your opposition in England, you will scarcely find a reception here, much less in France." He also noted: "You need not fear the coming of Alençon into this country: if he comes at all, it will hardly be before autumn; and if you should follow the camp only for a few months, you would derive great advantage from it." Then on March 12 he wrote: "I wonder why the Duke of Anjou has conceived this dislike of you. If he hates you only because you opposed him in England, he will soon be reconciled to you, and it will be unnecessary for you to say more than that you acted, not from ill-will towards him, but for the good of the your country. You gain neither advantage nor honor by quarreling with men of his rank." While Sidney's replies to these letters are lost, his attitude may easily be inferred from that of Languet. The translations are those of S. A. Pears, *The Correspondence of Philip Sidney and Hubert Languet* (London, 1845). For Languet's role in mediating the 1580 agreement between Orange and Anjou, see Appendix A.

from Languet, its engineer, few could muster confidence in such an ally at that point. By his death in 1581 Languet was spared from seeing Anjou betray the Protestants once again, this time in the "furie française" of January 1583 wherein Anjou attempted an armed takeover of Antwerp. Chased ignominiously from the Low Countries and discarded by the Huguenots once and for all, Anjou languished in France until his death in 1584. How much if any of this later history percolates into *New Arcadia*, which also belongs to 1584, is unclear, although Anjou's deathbed repudiation of his rebellious behavior[22] may have suggested the similar repudiation made by the chastened Amphialus moments before his attempted suicide (1:493). But *New Arcadia* is not topical allegory, and Amphialus, if partially inspired by Anjou, transcends him as well in a manner to be clarified shortly; my point here is that by 1584 the self-serving nature of that "subaltern magistrate" in whom Languet's *Vindiciae* had invested much of its hopes was fully patent, and the faulty marriage between personal ambition and disinterested resistance ripe for generalization in fiction.

[4]

The "bare *was*" of history calls for transfiguration by the poet, if poetry is in fact to be more "philosophical" than history, as Sidney, following Aristotle, insists it should.[23] We must now observe the changes Sidney effects in his material—for whatever survives into *New Arcadia* directly indicative of Anjou is fairly incidental—and demand their rationale.

First, by reporting Amphialus' "justification" in the third person, Sidney establishes esthetic distance between the upstart's position and that of the narrator. Amphialus' position, that is to say, is not trustworthy but suffers correction at every turn by the normative voice of the narrator, who, as we have seen, reminds us of the dyslogistic nature of the rebel argument. Thus we are often able to appreciate a discrepancy between Amphialus' assertions and the true nature of the case (whatever Sidney felt toward Henry III's

---

[22]Cf. Jacques Berson, *Regret funebre contenant les actions et derniers propos de Monseigneur, fils de France, frere unique du Roy, depuis sa maladie iusques a son trespas* (1584).

[23]Philip Sidney, *Apology for Poetry*, ed. Geoffry Shepheard (London: Nelson, 1965), p. 109-10.

Italianate advisers, for example, the Arcadian Philanax's stew-
ardship of the state clearly does not deserve Amphialus' censure).
Similarly, it may be significant that Sidney causes the rebellion to
originate principally with the unrelievedly wicked Cecropia rather
than with her more complex son (Anjou's rebellion, in contrast,
owed nothing to his mother). By making these changes, Sidney
clarifies his adverse judgment of the monarchomach argument.
However praiseworthy in the abstract, this argument never functions in *Arcadia* as anything other than ideological cover for a self-
serving rebel. For the poet does not condemn Amphialus only to
advance a more virtuous monarchomach in his place; the point is
not that he is a defective version of an ideal rebel but that the ideal of
rebellion itself is flawed, a "false application" of the argument for
normative rule.

To emphasize this ironic marriage between a sententious ideal and
its corrupt use, Sidney modifies history on another point. He causes
the rebel himself directly to enunciate the justificatory theory of the
subaltern magistrate on the eve of his revolt, whereas the cognate
document, Anjou's *Protestation,* while it argues for the rule of law,
does not draw explicitly on that technical item. The title of "subaltern magistrate" accrued to Anjou thanks to the formal works contributed to his cause by other men.[24] By allowing Amphialus himself to draw directly on this key item, Sidney conflates into a single
revolutionary manifesto the entire cluster of documents generated
by the 1575-1576 rebellion, ranging from the most occasional and
blatantly self-serving (that *Protestation* published by the primary
rebel himself) to that which was ostensibly the most disinterested
(Languet's scrupulous and learned *Vindiciae*). The effect, I think, is
to unmask the partisan nature of the doctrine of the subaltern.
While a work such as Languet's *Vindiciae* pretended to lofty ideals,
ultimately it served (Sidney would seem to suggest) merely as window dressing for the aims of a limited individual or group. Thus
Sidney evaluates the monarchomach argument less by condemning

---

[24]Anjou did not have to wait long for this title. Innocent Gentillet anonymously
published at Geneva in 1576 an edition of Anjou's *Protestation* replete with a lengthy
critical apparatus vaunting Anjou as a "subaltern magistrate"; cf. *Brieve remonstrance a
la noblesse de la France sur le faict de la Declaration de Mgr le duc d'Alençon* (1576). In
referring to the "glosses of probabilitie" which adorn the copies of Amphialus' manifesto (1:371), Sidney may have in mind Gentillet's sixty-some pages of glosses.

it explicitly than by demonstrating its partisan motives, its substructure of interest.

Whether Sidney's adverse judgment of the monarchomachs is just is a question that should perhaps be reserved for the historian. But I should point out that modern historians have in some ways confirmed this judgment. Only recently have they demanded the *cui bono?* of the monarchomach works; these turn out to be less disinterested than was believed by Whig historians of earlier generations. Thus it was not until 1969 that Languet's *Vindiciae*, finally disabused of its anonymous, theoretical air and located in its historical context, was shown to have the most intimate relationship to the Anjou-Condé-Casimir axis and the 1575-1576 revolt against Henry III.[25] By collapsing the primary ideological item of the *Vindiciae*—the doctrine of the subaltern—into the personal manifesto of the Anjou cognate, Sidney may be said to have anticipated this conclusion of modern scholarship. For good or ill, and whether or not inadvertently, Languet's argument was as much the creature of the renegade nobility centering on Anjou as the monarchomach argument in Sidney's *New Arcadia* is that of Amphialus.

Sidney makes another major change in his raw material, one that may seem to undermine his general tendency to judge adversely the fictional rebellion. While he condemns Amphialus *qua* rebel, it is true that he elsewhere depicts him in terms that are not unfavorable. In fact, apart from the rebellion episode, this knight functions as something of a chivalric paragon, if at times a juvenile one. Thus Sidney often allows the reader of *New Arcadia* to feel far more sympathy for Amphialus, "excellent son of an evill mother" (1:363), than he does for Cecropia, once appointing Amphialus, for example, "such a right manlike man, as Nature often erring, yet shewes she would fain make" (1:222-23). If the fictional rebellion owes something to Anjou's and is judged accordingly, the Amphialus portrait insofar as positive signals Sidney's divergence from that model— whose appeal to Sidney was nil—and we must ask why he should have chosen to rehabilitate the rebel at all. Yet as we shall see, even the otherwise positive portrait of Amphialus enables the poet to drive home all the more truly his reasoned condemnation of Amphialus *qua* monarchomach.

[25]This was the contribution of Mastellone, op cit.

[5]

At this point, Richard McCoy's *Sir Philip Sidney: Rebellion in Arcadia* (1979) enables me to complete the argument of this chapter. McCoy's study concerns rebellion less in the political than in the psychological sense; thus it is not part of his purpose to investigate Sidney's relationship to the monarchomachs, who figure only in passing. He helps us by engaging the question of Sidney's ambiguity with respect to Amphialus. He feels that the poet's handling of Amphialus is marked by authorial evasiveness and irresolution for which Sidney's ambiguous feeling before the category of rebellion would be responsible. "Sidney was obviously intrigued with [the subaltern magistrate] theory because he was himself a frustrated subaltern, but its transparently subversive nature prompts him to drop the subject almost as soon as it comes up."[26] Yet the poet's reasoned objection to Amphialus' rebellion amounts neither to dropping the subject nor to evading it. While McCoy has a good discussion of the various inconsistencies in Amphialus' "justification," he seems to speak as if these inconsistencies were Sidney's own, whereas the poet seems to me to be fully in control of Amphialus' equivocations and "false applications." Similarly, McCoy feels that Sidney—to whom we owe a devastating portrait of Amphialus' romantic and chivalric compulsiveness, eventual self-abasement before his mother and other women, and inability either to obey or to revolt with any success—should be censured for the same qualities.[27] It may be true that Sidney, refused a significant position by Elizabeth, was, if you like, a "frustrated subaltern." Yet I wonder whether McCoy has not unjustly transferred the acute sense of division that undeniably marks Amphialus (whose name means "between two seas") to his creator. Does the duplicitous nature of Amphialus' portrait result from the poet's unresolved attitude toward his material or does it possess fictional logic?

What Sidney shares in common with Amphialus and the monarchomachs is membership in the warrior aristocracy. It was this class, as Michael Walzer has shown, to which the king-fighters appealed and which provided the primary energy of their opposition to the monarchy. Themselves noblemen and retainers of nobles, the

---

[26]McCoy, p. 58.
[27]McCoy, pp. 182–89.

Huguenot publicists provided a means whereby the great lords rendered insecure by the centralizing trend of the century might regain their feudal status. The primary duty of the nobility, Languet insists, "is to fight the enemies of the nation . . . the recompense of the fatigue and danger to which the nobles are exposed is the honor granted them by the other orders of the state."[28] Thus Languet's *Vindiciae* rebaptizes *le preux* — the gallant knight — as the *regni procer,* "strong man of the kingdom"; bestows upon him constitutional status as *regni officarius,* "subaltern magistrate"; and reserves rebellion as a privilege exclusively of the aristocracy. "Huguenot theory," concludes Walzer, "may be considered an unsuccessful effort to transform feudal status into constitutional position."[29] And in the 1570s the renegade French nobility makes its principal bid for power in the 1575-1576 rebellion before being disciplined by the Valois monarchy.

Now while Sidney may nominally have been a member of the warrior aristocracy, he did not necessarily share all of its centrifugal impulses. In fact Sidney regarded the aristocratic cult of martial "courage" with the utmost suspicion, and his skeptical attitude toward this cult generates much of the ironic energy of both *Arcadias.* Though perhaps to different ends, his fiction develops an attitude toward the warrior ethic that is no less ironic than that of Cervantes. *Arcadia* locates the medieval warrior in a modern sixteenth-century monarchy; and to Sidney the warrior who does not subserve the purposes of the newer and larger political unit regularly becomes sentimental, funny, indulgent, out of place, and profoundly dangerous. Amphialus' policy of challenging all comers in single combat proves as politically reckless as it seems admirable, and subversive even of his own cause. When he insists on fighting Phalantus, "his olde governour with persuasions mingled with reprehensions (that he would rather affect the glorie of a private fighter, then of a wise Generall) . . . [seeks] . . . to dissuade him" (1:414). Affecting such "private" glory inevitably spells trouble. When Philanax's brother, "neither staying the commandement of the captaine, nor recking whether his face were armed," charges Amphialus "as if the marke had been but a ring, & the lookers on Ladies," his opponent

[28]Cf. Henri Chevreul, *Hubert Languet* (1852; reprinted, Nieuwkoop: B. De Graaf, 1967), pp. 115–16.
[29]Walzer, p. 73.

inadvertently spears him in the face and wounds him mortally, thereby aggravating the Arcadian war (1:387)—a throwaway allusion to Montgomery's similar killing of Henry II at a 1559 tournament,[30] but more significantly a neat exemplum suggesting the political consequences of releasing the *preux* on his own trajectory. Sidney had only to look at twenty years of civil warfare in France to appreciate the danger of a theory that justifies rebellion by any trigger-happy nobleman. It is the "principall men in honor and might" who begrudge Philanax his advancement (4:300), fuel Amphialus' rebellion, stir up the "popular sort" (e.g., 1:32ff, 4:305), and whom—with the entire approval of the narrator—the exemplary monarch, Euarchus, must severely discipline to secure peace in his kingdom (1:184ff). Sidney's most involved essay in the dangers of a strong-headed nobility is the Amphialus episode, since this prince owes his chivalric belligerence (as well as his ideas about love) to the warrior ethic. Here as elsewhere in *Arcadia*, we must appreciate the appeal of this code in order to understand its dangers. And so Amphialus must be represented as a "right manlike man" sufficiently misguided to turn his considerable talents in the wrong direction. What ambiguity obtains in the episode does not seem to me to concern the poet's evaluation of rebellion; nor does it seem without design. It is entirely functional, insofar as it enables us to define Amphialus' rebelliousness as the obverse of his martial enthusiasm. Sidney plays a generic literary figure of perennial charm (the knight) off against the exigencies of monarchic politics. Amphialus is politically dangerous for the same reason that he is generically attractive.

Thus Amphialus results from Sidney's reasoned synthesis of a historical actor (François d'Anjou) with a conventional literary-historical figure (the feudal warrior). While the poet thereby sacrifices any merely topical reference, he clarifies and generalizes his critique of the monarchomachs. Indeed his synthesis anticipates and lends credence to Walzer's analysis of the overlap between the Huguenots' "subaltern magistrate" and the feudal warrior. The great Huguenot noble La Noue admitted that the medieval romances of *Amadis* still caused "un esprit de vertige" among the men

---

[30] As noticed by Marcus Goldman, *Sir Philip Sidney and the Arcadia* (Urbana: University of Illinois Press, 1934), pp. 168–69.

of his generation;[31] and Sidney seems to echo him in the *Apology for Poetry:* "Truly, I have known men, that even with reading *Amadis de Gaule* (which God knoweth wanteth much of a perfect poesy) have found their hearts moved to the exercise of courtesy, liberality, and especially courage."[32] Yet where the *Vindiciae* depends on the feudal warrior as an agent of reformation, Sidney regards him as potentially seditious. Every "great Lord" is potentially a "little king" (1:185) threatening to install his own self-sufficient locus of authority. Thus Sidney's *Arcadia* appropriates material from *Amadis* and similar romances but in order to reconstruct it with urbane monarchic vigilance.[33]

We misconceive Sidney's linkage of monarchomach energies with chivalric if we suppose it results from a desire to vindicate either aspect of the synthesis: it is systematic, has excellent sociological warrant, and should be considered of a piece with his general scrutiny throughout *Arcadia* of the warrior ethic. As for the suggestion that Amphialus "undoubtedly bears in some particulars a striking resemblance to Sidney himself,"[34] this is not untenable if we qualify it to mean that, like Amphialus, Sidney could have been employed more profitably than he was. Sidney thus accords Amphialus a degree of dignity that the Valois model never possessed in his eyes and perhaps a degree of power that he himself never acquired, but only by way of generalizing this subaltern's appeal, involving us in his mistake, and demonstrating the greater corruption of a finer thing: *corruptio optimi pessima.*

Despite his ultimate condemnation of the resistance rhetoric of the 1570s, it is important to note that Sidney was nourished on such rhetoric. Although eventually weaned from it, he preserves in 1584 a certain nostalgia for its simplicities and allows himself to suggest its attractiveness even while insisting on its dangers. It proves impossible for Sidney to dissociate himself entirely from those ideas that he has intersected in so many different ways, thanks to his ties with Hotman, Estienne, Marnix, Orange, and Languet. None of these

---

[31]Cf. François de La Noue, *Discours politiques et militaires* (1612), pp. 133–147.
[32]Sidney, p. 114.
[33]For Sidney's many borrowings from *Amadis*, cf. R. W. Zandvoort, *Sidney's Arcadia* (Amsterdam, 1929), pp. 193–195.
[34]Kenneth Myrick, *Sir Philip Sidney as a Literary Craftsman* (2nd ed.; Lincoln: University of Nebraska Press, 1965), p. 237.

friendships is lost on him. They leave small but detectable traces in his fiction—that line of the sonnet sequence *Astrophil and Stella,* "No kings be crown'd, but they some covenants make";[35] that passage of the *Apology for Poetry* which notes noncommitally, "Philosophy teacheth [that tyrants] *occidendos esse*";[36] that praise of Hubert Languet in *Old Arcadia,* which remains to challenge us; and finally, not so small or cryptic a trace, Book III of *New Arcadia.* Recreating the prototypal monarchomach encounter between the "subaltern magistrate" and his sovereign, Sidney invests the rebelling effort with the sense of farce that he feels its historical inspiration deserves, and the sense of tragic misdirection that he realizes it surely did not.

---

[35]*Astrophil and Stella* 69, in William A. Ringler (ed.), *The Poems of Sir Philip Sidney* (Oxford: Clarendon Press, 1962), p. 200.
   [36]Sidney, p. 112.

CHAPTER THREE

War in Sparta

And let not man examine this by booke,
As states stand paynted, or enammeld there
— Fulke Greville

[1]

ONE WAY OF DESCRIBING SIDNEY'S ATTITUDE toward the liberal
political tradition of which the monarchomachs form a part is
to say that he considers its doctrines attractive in theory but defective
in practice. In the first version of the fiction the apparent death of
King Basilius throws Arcadia into confusion. "Altogether like a falling steeple, the partes whereof, as windowes, stones, and pinnacles,
were well, but the whole mass ruinous." When various suggestions
are made concerning the future disposition of the state, the narrator categorically condemns those who suggest fitting Arcadia with
a republican rather than a monarchic polity:

> For some there were that cried to have the state altered, and gov-
> erned no more by a Prince; marry in the alteration, many would
> have the *Lacedemonian* government of few chosen Senatours;
> others the *Athenian*, where the peoples voyce helde the chiefe auc-
> thoritye. *But they were rather the discoursing sort of men, then the active,*
> [*such republicanism*] *being a matter more in imaginacion then practise*
> (2:131, my emphasis; cf. 4:300).

Conversely, those receive the narrator's approbation who recognize
that Arcadia, a country that "knewe no government, without a
Prince," should choose and submit to a monarch once again; and
indeed the return of social order in Arcadia must await the restora-
tion of monarchy. Sidney, then, presents the republican models,

39

whether Lacedemonian aristocracy or Athenian democracy, as
adequate to the abstract discussions of book-learned men—"rather
the discoursing sort of men, then the active"—but as irrelevant to
concrete practice, or at least to "the present case" of Arcadia.

Until Sidney's time political discussion was often referred automatically to classical models. Indeed it was difficult to think about
politics at all without thinking in terms developed by the classical
masters. In the poet's time, no better representative of the classicizing political style obtains than the monarchomachs. For in seeking to
limit the burgeoning power of the king, the monarchomachs adduce the traditional battery of arguments and exempla in favor of
the *status mixtus* from Polybius, Aristotle, and Cicero. But about the
end of the sixteenth century a number of thinkers, of which Sidney is
only one, begin to suspect that the classicizing idiom and models
cannot provide guidance to the problems of a political quantity un-
known in the ancient world, namely, the nation-state, and to seek
actively for some kind of alternative way of talking about politics.
The traditional terms and models may well have made sense in their
original context of the city-state, and perhaps still make sense in the
context of the republics of the Italian Renaissance (where they
thrive in the hands of such practitioners as Guicciardini, Contarini,
and Machiavelli), but these critics feel that they cannot legitimately
be applied to such centralized monarchies as England, France, and
Arcadia, countries that "[know] no government, without a Prince."
In the 1584 *New Arcadia,* then, Sidney will develop his earlier brief
critique of the traditional terms and models. I shall begin by review-
ing what may be called the classicist claims for Sparta, and then I
shall turn to the poet's disconfirmation of these claims in *New Arcadia.*

[2]

Ancient Sparta (what Sidney terms Lacedemonia or, using the
syncopated Roman form, Laconia) occurs regularly throughout the
libertarian political tradition as a historical exemplar of one of its
favorite ideals, the mixed state. Like ancient Athens or republican
Rome, Sparta is considered by the libertarians to provide a historical
illustration of that political arrangement best securing the rule of
law—the *status mixtus*—and it figures as such in the monarchomachs.

The Spartan myth, by which I mean the exemplaristic use of this state, goes back principally to Polybius, Plato, and Plutarch. According to Plutarch, Sparta achieved stability with Lycurgus' institution of a senate, "which he made to have a regall power and equall authoritie with the Kings in matters of weight and importance, and it was (as Plato sayeth) to be the healthfull counterpease of the whole bodye of the Common weale."[1] Before Lycurgus' institution of this senate, Sparta was "ever wavering, sometime inclining to tyrannie, when the Kings were to mightie: and sometime to confusion, when the people would usurpe authoritie."[2] Lycurgus' reform thus created a *système équilibré*, holding in peaceful, temperate mixture the three pure kinds of government recognized by the classical theorists, with the senate (the Gerousia or council of elders) representing aristocracy, the ephors (magistrates appointed from the Spartan community specifically for the purpose of overseeing the kings) representing democracy, and the curious Spartan institution of double kingship representing monarchy. Since the "kinds" of government, apart from the executive, corresponded to the two principal social classes, Lycurgus' prescription guaranteed social harmony. Here in ancient Sparta, then, was a historical illustration of the virtues of the "mixed state." In such a state, opposed interests so balance themselves as to prevent any single one from usurping power. Since no one of the three different loci can, at least in theory, entirely escape the limitations posed by the other two, the rule of law is ensured—the rule of reason, that is to say, as opposed to the rule of some arbitrary interest, will, or class.

Plutarch's praise of the Lycurgan system—"the government of Sparta seemed not to be a policy or common weal, but rather a certain holy place and order of religion"[3]—is representative of the praise of Sparta throughout the mixed state theorists. Innumerable writers in the libertarian tradition all the way to Jean-Jacques Rousseau thus prosecute what may be called the "Spartan myth." In the Renaissance, the Plutarchan encomium of ancient Sparta is echoed, for example, by Contarini, Giannotti, Machiavelli, and Paruta among the Italians; by Ponet, Harrington, Algernon Sydney, and Milton among the English; and by Beza and Languet among the French. Their concern over what they saw as the encroachments of

---

[1] Plutarch, *Lives of the Noble Grecians and Romanes Translated by Sir Thomas North* (Oxford: Basil Blackwell, 1928), p. 114.
[2] Ibid., p. 114.
[3] Ibid., p. 156.

the Valois dynasty led the monarchomachs to rely heavily on the theory of the mixed state. Especially was Sparta important for the monarchomachs since Calvin himself, in an important passage of the *Institutes*, had drawn attention to the Spartan ephorate as an example of a constitutional safeguard on the king's rapacity.[4]

It is true that a mixed system such as the Spartan allows, at least theoretically, for a monarchic element in addition to aristocracy and democracy. But the theory of mixed government inevitably tended to become part of the arsenal of opponents to monarchy, whether Valois, Marian, or Stuart. As Zera Fink notes, two factors made this a natural development. First, the classical mixed state placed far greater restrictions on the monarch than any sixteenth century royalist was prepared to admit. The classical debate ultimately reduced to the question of how power should be apportioned between the aristocratic and the democratic elements; it hardly occurred to them to think of investing any real power in the royal element, which was rarely conceived as having anything more than an adjudicative function at best. Second, the theory of the mixed state was compatible with a concept of armed resistance to royal abuse and even of tyrannicide.[5]

If king-fighters found Sparta and the mixed state attractive, royalists eventually did not. This does not mean that all royalists were absolutists or wished to dispense entirely with a system of limitations on royal prerogative. Many of them simply felt that a theory cut to the modest measure of a city-state threw little if any light on the great monarchies of the sixteenth century. The nation-state that had evolved as a result of the centralizing efforts of Louis XI in France and Thomas Cromwell in England displayed a dynamic that ancient discussion had no way of anticipating. Thus a number of royalists ruled out Sparta from this discussion on monarchy by noting that the Spartan kingship bore no more than a nominal resemblance to modern monarchy: "inane regum nomen erat"; the Spartan kings, as even ancient writers noted, were not real kings.[6] It

---

[4]*Institutes* (1559 ed.) 4.20.31. Thus Hubert Languet, A *Defense of Liberty Against Tyrants* (1924; reprinted, Gloucester, Mass: Peter Smith, 1963); pp. 129, 136, 148, 176; See also Theodore Beza, *Du droit des magistrats*, ed. Robert M. Kingdon (Geneva: Droz, 1971), p. 28.

[5]Cf. Zera S. Fink, *The Classical Republicans* (2nd ed.; Evanston: Northwestern University Press, 1962), pp. 24–26.

[6]Cf. Adam Blackwood, *Adversus Georgii Buchanani dialogum . . . pro regibus apologia* (1581); also William Barclay, *De regno et regali potestate* (1600), who refers approvingly

was difficult, however, to question the mixed state without striking at the heart of classical political thought. It took a thinker of the originality of Jean Bodin to suggest that the doctrine of mixture or balance was not only irrelevant to sixteenth century monarchy but also inherently self-contradictory, since even in the classical city-states the actual dynamic of power presupposed a tilt toward one element or another of the "mixture." Thus Bodin noticed that even the historical Sparta did not correspond to the theoretical mixed state; rather power shifted back and forth between the two components of the mixture, being now located in patrician hands and now in plebeian.[7] This was also the procedure of another critic of the Spartan myth—Philip Sidney. By developing some indications that already existed in the classical writers, Sidney arrived at a picture of Sparta that bore little resemblance to the sentimentalized libertarian portrait. So far from being "a certain holy place and order of religion," Sidney's is an anti-Sparta, a chronically dysfunctional state. Not only, then, is the Spartan ideal inapplicable to the "present case" of modern centralized monarchy; it doesn't even work in Sparta itself. Sidney thus contrives to make one of the favorite historical exemplars of the classicizing theorists testify against rather than for the rule of law.

[3]

Apart from that one reference to the "Lacedemonian government of few chosen Senatours" which the narrator contemptuously dismisses as good for books but not practice, Sparta does not figure in the *Old Arcadia*. In the revised version, however, the very first pages bear on Spartan politics.

The *New Arcadia* begins as Musidorus is cast up on the shores of the Peloponnesus. The shepherds Claius and Strephon revive him and then escort him through Laconia (Lacedemonia) until he reaches Arcadia. (That is, they travel north through Laconia, which occupies the southern half of the Peloponnesus, to reach the land-

---

to Cornelius Nepos' observation that the Spartan kings "were not real kings" (see Elizabeth Rawson, *The Spartan Tradition in European Thought* [Oxford: Clarendon Press, 1969], pp. 164–165). Nepos' observation is also quoted approvingly in Grotius, *De jure belli ac pacis* (1625) 1.3.8.11.
[7] Jean Bodin, *La République* (1576) 2.1.

locked state of Arcadia.) Upon reaching Arcadia, Musidorus ex-
presses surprise at the contrast between the "wasted soile" of
Laconia and the delightful hills and valleys of Arcadia. The reason
for this difference lies in contemporary politics, as the shepherds
inform him:

> The country . . . where you were cast ashore, & now are past
> through, is Laconia, not so poore by the barrennes of the soyle
> (though in it selfe not passing fertill) as by a civil warre, which
> being these two yeares within the bowels of that estate, betweene
> the gentlemen & the peasants (by them named *Helots*) hath in this
> sorte as it were disfigured the face of nature, and made it so un-
> hospitall as now you have found it: the townes neither of the one
> side nor the other, willingly opening their gates to strangers, nor
> strangers willingly entring for fear of being mistaken (1:14).

In contrast to the Laconian situation, Arcadia is "decked with
peace," though the reason why civil war has wasted Laconia while
being averted in Arcadia is not yet suggested.

But soon Laconian affairs spill over into Arcadia when the son of
Musidorus' Arcadian host is captured by the Helots. As Musidorus
(now called Palladius) will go to Laconia to help rescue Clitophon, he
desires to know something more about the wars there and the "partie against whom . . . he was to fight." "A man well acquainted with
the affaires of Laconia" informs him that the Helots

> were a kinde of people, who having been of old, freemen and
> possessioners, the Lacedemonians had conquered them, and layd,
> not onely tribute, but bondage upon them: which they had long
> borne; till of late the *Lacedemonians* through greedinesse growing
> more heavie then they could beare, and through contempt lesse
> carefull how to make them beare, they had with a generall consent
> (rather springing by the generalnes of the cause, then of any ar-
> tificiall practise) set themselves in armes, and whetting their cour-
> age with revenge, and grounding their resolution upon despaire,
> they had proceeded with unlooked-for succes: having already
> taken divers Towns and Castels, with the slaughter of many of the
> gentrie; for whom no[r] sex nor age could be accepted for an
> excuse.

Although at first the Helots fought with mere "beastlie furie," practice has now made them

comparable to the best of the *Lacedemonians;* & more of late then
ever; by reason, first of *Demagoras* a great Lord, who had made him
self of their partie, and since his death, of an other Captaine they
had gotten, who had brought up their ignorance, and brought
downe their furie, to such a meane of good government, and withall so valourouslie, that . . . they had the better in some . . . great
conflicts: in such wise, that the estate of *Lacedaemon* had sent unto
them, offering peace with most reasonable and honorable conditions (1:39).

The Laconian "civil warre" between gentlemen and Helots goes on
for some time, now with a contingent from Arcadia including
Musidorus interfering on behalf of the gentlemen. Now it happens
that the new "Captain" of the Helots mentioned in the last-quoted
passage, who has brought them to "a meane of good government," is
Musidorus' best friend, Pyrocles, the other hero of Sidney's *Arcadia*.
When the two friends recognize each other, they immediately halt
the fighting and arrange a truce. It is important to note that only the
two heroes' personal friendship has put an end to the Laconian civil
war. And the situation may not be permanently stabilized since
neither hero—Musidorus for the gentlemen and Pyrocles for the
Helots—is a native of Laconia but has only lent his services temporarily; indeed one of the truce articles that the gentlemen insist on
is that Pyrocles "no more tarry" with the Helots. Pyrocles represents
to the Helots the truce he has negotiated for them with the
Lacedemonian kings[8] and nobility, "which is in all points as your
selves desired," and prepares to relinquish his leadership:

> The Townes and Fortes you presently have, are still left unto you,
> to be kept either with or without garrison, so as you alter not the
> lawes of the Countrie, and pay such dueties as the rest of the
> Laconians doo. Your selves are made by publique decree, free
> men, and so capable both to give and receive voice in election of
> Magistrates. The distinction of names between *Helots* and
> *Lacedemonians* to be quite taken away, and all indifferently to enjoy
> both names and priviledges of *Laconians*. Your children to be
> brought up with theirs in *Spartane* discipline: and so you (framing
> your selves to be good members of that estate) to be hereafter
> fellowes, and no longer servaunts (1:46-47).

[8]Sidney knew from Plutarch of the Lacedemonian double kingship; thus the
plural. But he is not entirely consistent on this point, occasionally referring to a single
king.

The Helots are not uniformly satisfied with the terms of this truce, and would prefer "rather to try the uttermost event, then to lose him by whom they had beene victorious," that is, Pyrocles. But Pyrocles "as well with generall orations, as particular dealing with the men of most credit, made them thoroughly see how necessary it was to preferre such an opportunity before a vain affection; but yet could not prevaile, till openly he sware, that he would (if at any time the *Lacedemonians* brake this treatie) come back again, and be their captaine" (1:47). The heroes, Pyrocles and Musidorus, both quit Laconia and return to Arcadia, and this is—almost—the last we hear of the Spartan or Laconian situation because the intrigue shifts elsewhere for the rest of the *New Arcadia*.

But not quite. We know that, as he continued the revision, Sidney intended to return to Laconia. For the 1593 folio produced by Mary Sidney, the composite version which fills out the fragmentary revision with narrative material from Books III through V of the old version, contains new information on the Helots. This is possible because the (now lost) manuscript of the old version that Mary Sidney drew on for the 1593 edition was not exactly identical to the manuscripts of that work Feuillerat (1912) and Robertson (1973) published. Many of the changes in Books III through V of the old version as printed in 1593 were simply introduced by the editor in order to bring the last part of the old narrative into conformity with the revised first part, but nonetheless there are two passages containing a considerable amount of rewriting, and William Ringler has shown that these two episodes could only have been written by Sidney himself. Thus the narrative portion of the last three books of the 1593 folio "preserves several additional pages of Sidney's own composition and gives us some imperfect hints of how he intended to continue his revision of the story."[9] Now both of these additional episodes are closely linked by a reference in each to a second uprising of the Helots. The first new episode concerns Pyrocles' visit to Philoclea's bedchamber, and the second, Euarchus' journey to Arcadia. Each contains some four pages of completely new material representing a continuation of intrigue in the published *New Arcadia*.

In the earlier version of the poem Pyrocles goes to Philoclea's

[9]William A. Ringler (ed.), *The Poems of Sir Philip Sidney* (Oxford: Clarendon Press, 1962), pp. 377–78.

bedchamber "to satisfy his greedy desyer" (4:215). In the 1593 folio, he plans instead to elope with her to Laconia, where they may receive protection from the Helots:

> The same daye, I saye, she [i.e., Pyrocles, disguised as a woman] resolved on a way to rid out of the lodge her two combersome lovers, and in the night to carrie away *Philoclea:* where unto she was assured her owne love, no lesse than her sisters, woulde easely winne her consent. Hoping that although their abrupt parting had not suffered her to demaund of *Musidorus* which way he ment to direct his journey, yet either they should by some good fortune, finde him: or if that course fayled, yet they might well recover some towne of the *Helotes,* near the frontieres of *Arcadia,* who being newly againe up in armes against the Nobilitie, she knew would bee as glad of her presence, as she of their protection (2:41-42).

While this is not the only piece of rewriting in the new bedchamber visit, we learn here that the peace arranged by the two heroes at the beginning of *New Arcadia* has not held because the Helots are "newly againe up in armes against the Nobilitie."

The second major piece of new writing, concerning Euarchus' visit to Arcadia, is more explicit about the current Helot situation including the breaking of the truce and the new revolt. In the *Old Arcadia,* when Sidney's ideal king, Euarchus of Macedon, hears of Basilius' retirement, he decides to visit him and sails directly to the "Arcadian shore," landing at "a porte not far from" the principal Arcadian city of Mantinea (4:331-33). In the 1593 addition, Euarchus has no project to sail to Arcadia. Having fortified the western coast of Macedonia to prevent an invasion from Italy, he agrees to aid Queen Erona, who is imprisoned in Armenia, and accordingly sails for Byzantium to raise a force for her release. But as his ships sail southward down what is now the Adriatic and around the Peloponnesus, they encounter "an extreme tempest" and are "so scattered, that scarcely any two [are] lefte together."

> As for the Kings owne shippe, deprived of all company, sore brused, and weatherbeaten, able no longer to brooke the seas churlish entertainment, a little before day it recovered the shore. The first light made them see it was the unhappy coast of Laconia: for no other country could have shown the like evidence of unnatural war. Which having long endured betweene the nobilitie and the *Helotes,* and once compounded by *Pyrocles,* under the name of

Daiphantus, immediately upon his departure had broken out more violently than ever before. For the King taking the opportunity of their captaines absence, refused to performe the condicions of peace, as extorted from him by rebellious violence. Whereupon they were againe deepely entred into warre, with so notable an hatred towardes the very name of a King, that *Euarchus* (though a straunger unto them) thought it not safe there to leave his person, where neither his owne force could be a defence, nor the sacred name of Majestie, a protection. Therefore calling to him an *Arcadian* . . . he demaunded of him the next place of suretie, where he might make his staye, until he might heare somewhat of his fleet, or cause his ship to be repaired (2:151-52).

The Arcadian gentleman, "glad to have the occasion of doing service to Euarchus, and honour to Basilius," offers to guide Euarchus through the hostile Laconian territory to his own king; and thus Euarchus is in Arcadia for the denouement of the romance.

From these two episodes, the only substantial passages of new writing we possess from the later books, we learn that one of Sidney's principal intentions is to point up the instability of the truce between Helots and gentlemen arranged by Pyrocles and Musidorus in the opening pages of the revision. It seems that immediately upon Pyrocles' departure from Laconia, "unnatural war . . . had broken out more violently than ever before." In fact, with the second Helot rebellion, Laconian affairs have been returned to exactly the same state they were in when Musidorus was first cast ashore on a Laconia "disfigured" by "civill war." Euarchus' shipwreck and voyage inland in the company of the "Arcadian gentleman" seems to echo Musidorus' opening shipwreck and voyage inland in the company of Strephon and Claius. Sidney's last piece of writing takes us back to the first scene of the *New Arcadia,* thus closing a circle, if a desperate one. Laconian affairs seem trapped in an endless, hopeless flux of rebellion, truce, rebellion.

[4]

Previous students of Sidney's Spartan or Laconian episode have been misled, I think, by focussing on the question of whether the poet considered the Helot revolt to be a legitimate one. Briggs and Bergbusch use the Helot revolt as part of their brief for a monarchomach Sidney, for here, they claim, is a rebellion of which Sidney approves. For Ribner, whether Sidney approves of the Helot revolt doesn't bear on monarchomach theory since there is no analogy between the attempt of the Helots, a formerly free people, to throw off the yoke of their oppressors and the condition of civil rebellion which the *Vindiciae* endorses under certain conditions as a means to the elimination of tyranny. Goldman has a third view: the Helot revolt is simply that of slaves against gentlemen, and Sidney does not approve of it at all.[10] My view is that Sidney is less concerned to praise or blame either one of the two classes involved in the civil war—the Helots or the gentlemen—than to pass judgment on the Spartan polity as a whole. Finally neither the Helots nor the gentlemen are at fault; it is Sparta as a unit that is somehow awry.

Sidney's civil wars come into focus as a disconfirmation of libertarian, exemplaristic Sparta. The poet calls the historical record—for his first fictional revolt clearly owes something to an incident of 464 B.C. in the course of which a contingent of Arcadian troops came to the aid of a Sparta besieged by revolting Helots[11]—to bear against the idealized "Spartan myth." Drawing on what might be called the minority report of ancient writers, Sidney broaches a problem that has always been a thorn in the side of ardent pro-Spartans. For it is difficult to reconcile the exemplaristic Plutarchan portrait of a fiercely freedom-loving state with that of a resident slave population kept in utter subjection. Where the libertarians preferred to forget this social paradox, Sidney insists on it.

As the classical writers agree, the Helots were a slave population kept in the strictest of bondage to the Spartans. Also traditional is Sidney's suggestion that the Helots were originally free: they were an Achaean people reduced to permanent slavery following the Dorian invasion of the Peloponnesus.[12] It is pointed out, in opposi-

---

[10]W. D. Briggs, "Political Ideas in Sidney's *Arcadia*," *SP* 28 (1931), pp. 140–141; See also Martin Bergbusch, "Political Thought and Conduct in Sidney's *Arcadia*," (Ph.D. dissertation, Cornell University, 1971), pp. 20–22, 236–245; Irving Ribner, "Machiavelli and Sidney: The 'Arcadia' of 1590," *SP* 57 (1950), 160–161; Irving Ribner, "Sir Philip Sidney on Civil Insurrection," *JHI* 13 (1952), 259–260; Marcus Goldman, *Sir Philip Sidney and the Arcadia* (Urbana: University of Illinois Press, 1934), pp. 169–73.

[11]Cf. Thucydides 1.101–03; Diodorus Siculus 11.63–64; Plutarch *Kim.* 16–17.3; Pausanias 1.28.8–9, 4.24.5–7; Xenophon *Hell.* 5.2.3.

[12]Plutarch *Lyc.* 2.1.

tion to sympathizers of the Spartan system, that the Helots, as a large resident slave population, represented a continual threat to the state: Thucydides and Plato write that the Helots could never forget their ancient liberty and thus posed a permanent danger to political stability.[13] Perhaps the most detailed analysis of the Helot problem is that of Aristotle in Book Two of the *Politics*, a work Sidney knew well. The Helots indicate a fundamental flaw in the Spartan system. The existence of such a subject slave class does not allow leisure for the citizens; rather it provides a continual source of anxiety:

> . . . there is always the need to be alert about how best to live with a subject population; if they are allowed too much license, they become full of themselves and begin to claim equal rights with their masters; if they are badly treated, they become resentful and rebellious. It is clear therefore that those who find themselves in such relations with their helotry have not yet found a solution to their problem.[14]

The chronic dread of a Helot insurrection led the Spartans to institute strict systems of supervision over them including the secret police called *crypteia*. Even Plutarch, who otherwise idealizes Sparta, notes ominously that every year the ephors formally declared war against the Helots in order that they might be killed without scruple.[15] Although the classical writers often blame Spartan severity toward the Helots, no one suggests that a Helot rebellion would mean anything but chaos. While Plato terms the Helot bondage the hardest in Greece, his own system of secret police is copied from that of the Spartans.[16] Should the Helots rise, Sparta falls.

Just back of the exemplaristic version of Sparta, then, lay a very different and even opposed picture—one that testified not to law but to chronic social and political anxiety, to a continual class war between a resident slave population and their increasingly strict overseers. So far from being peacefully counterpoised in the mixed state or *système équilibré* of theory, the two great opposing classes of sixth and fifth century Sparta were never at ease with each other and at the slightest provocation engaged in war, such as the Third Mes-

---

[13]Thucydides 4.26.80, 4.80.34, 5.64; Herodotus 9.28; Plato *Laws* 6.777C.
[14]Aristotle *Politics* 2.1269A, trans. T. A. Sinclair (Baltimore: Penguin Books, 1962). For Sidney's interest in this work, cf. his letter to Languet of Feb. 4, 1574.
[15]Plutarch *Lyc.* 28.
[16]Plato *Laws* 1.633B, 6.763A-C.

senian War of 464 B.C. during which the Spartans received support from Arcadian troops. By focussing on an incident such as this, and indeed by insisting throughout his episode on the anxiety-laden version of Sparta, Sidney discredits the Plutarchan or libertarian exemplar. Siding with the Greek historians and with Aristotle's *Politics* against Plutarch, the poet depicts Sparta as a *système déséquilibré* with no remedy in sight. It is true that in the fiction the Helots succeed in achieving the promise of integration with the Laconian gentlemen as a result of the truce negotiated by Pyrocles and Musidorus ("the distinction of names between *Helots* and *Lacedemonians* to be quite taken away, and all indifferently to enjoy both names and priviledges of *Laconians*"). The point here, however, is not so much whether the truce represents the establishment of something on the order of a mixed constitution, as a number of Sidney's critics have suggested,[17] but simply that it fails. For as soon as the two heroes absent themselves from Laconia, the two orders of Helots and gentlemen separate out again, like oil and water. Thus, particularly as a result of the 1593 passages, Sidney emphasizes not the triumph of the idea of integrity but its continual frustration.

Clearly the opening juxtaposition in *New Arcadia* of Sparta's "wasted soile" with Arcadia's "delightfull prospects" points a political lesson, where the republic suffers by contrast with the monarchy. Sidney thus disconfirms one of the cardinal republican items, according to which the rule of law presupposes a weakened executive. For Sidney as for other sixteenth century royalists a powerful monarch, so far from proving incompatible with peace, guarantees it. Sidney's greatest fear is indisputably the *rex inutilis* such as Basilius whose weakness and indecisiveness invite disorder; conversely, he indicates as his ideal the moderately absolute rule of Euarchus (= good king), who imperiously "thunder[s] a duetie into the subjects hartes" (1:186) by way of securing the rule of law.

The Spartan civil wars, then, demonstrate the results, according to Sidney, of diluting the monarchic element in the traditional republican manner. In the absence of a powerful sovereign after the fashion of Euarchus, Sparta dissolves into internecine warfare be-

---

[17]Cf. Bergbusch; also Rawson, p. 204. It should be noticed that Sidney's mixture differs appreciably from the traditional Spartan recipe, no one's conception of which allowed the Helots formal representation; as mere slaves, these were inferior even to the democratic element. Sidney, I think, concocts a more radical mixture of classes principally in order to watch it fall apart all the more decisively.

tween its two constituent social classes. It may be that from Sidney's
perspective, classical republicanism was at fault because it satisifed
itself with enumerating the two social estates and then simply postulating the submission of the lesser to the greater. I am not claiming
that Sidney, who considered it his "cheefest honor . . . to be a Dudlei," had any doubt about the difference between a gentleman and a
Helot. He did not. Precisely *because* lesser can never be made equal to
greater, both must seek mediation before an agency above and outside either one, namely, the monarch. Nor can one attempt to
mediate the dichotomy between greater and lesser simply by man-
dating that the two orders be melted into one, "the distinction of
names . . . to be quite taken away"—because the distinction between
the two orders is quite real and will inevitably surface, and no mere
change of names will abolish it. Insofar as this class distinction is an
ineluctable one, let both orders subject themselves to the monarch,
who, as Sidney notes, is ideally "law give[r], and law rule[r]" (2:194),
the "hopefull ende" to which all citizens greater as well as lesser
should be directed (1:186). Where classical republicanism sought a
principle of order *within* the social configuration, postulating the
"natural" submission of lesser to greater, Sidney seeks a principle of
order from *outside* the social configuration—the monarch. Thus he
agrees with the position of Richard Hooker and Grotius among his
contemporaries, who reject the Aristotelian argument according to
which the gentleman "naturally" presides over the commoner, and
argue instead that gentleman and commoner indifferently must
submit to the monarch.[18]

Sidney's reason for recalling the classical suggestion that the
Helots were once free is not to legitimize their rebellion—why
legitimize this one and yet dismiss that of the Phagonian commoners
with such aristocratic scorn (4:120ff)?—but rather to point up the
adventitious or "unnatural" aspect of the gentleman's dominion
over the Helot and thereby to suggest the partially adventitious
nature of any social hierarchy. Since society is an anxiously dynamic
entity, with the lesser laying claim to their primal freedom and the
greater refusing to grant it, extrinsic rule of a partially coercive
nature becomes necessary. Sidney's Sparta represents society without benefit of such an extrinsic coercive principle. The question as to

---

[18]Richard Hooker, *The Laws of Ecclesiastical Polity* 1.10.4; Grotius 1.3.8; Pufendorf,
The Whole Duty of Man 1.2.6, 2.6.7–9.

which side of the ensuing intestine warfare the poet prefers is irrelevant: he has apportioned his favors, and his heroes, fairly equally, assigning one to the Helots and the other to the gentlemen. His concern is not whether the Helots should rebel but that they will. They will rebel, the civil war will continue, until Sparta is rescued from its traditional republicanism by the vigorous intervention of such a monarch as Euarchus, whose timely measures save not only Macedonia (1:184ff) but Arcadia itself from collapsing into intestine warfare.

[5]

While in the *New Arcadia* Sidney examines one famous republican exemplum, he takes on another in a letter dating from 1578. Sidney's conclusion here agrees with that in the fiction and suggests one possible source for his skepticism with regard to the traditional political idiom.

Another common libertarian exemplum is Venice. It is a commonplace of Renaissance political discussion that this city provides a modern incarnation of the mixed state, with the Senate representing the element of aristocracy; the Council of Forty, the element of democracy; and the constitutionally crippled Doge, the element of monarchy. Sidney was quite familiar with the "Venetian myth"; indeed he read the Venetian humanists who gave it currency. Yet he eventually rejected it in terms that correlate closely with his rejection of the "Spartan myth." As a nineteen-year-old touring the continent in 1573, Sidney wrote Hubert Languet from Venice, recommending among a number of "really choice" books "*Il Stato di Vinegia,* written by [Gasparo] Contarini and Donato Giannotti" (3:81). Since Contarini and Giannotti (whose treatises were often bound as a single volume) represented two seminal proponents of the Venetian myth, Sidney was clearly familiar with it from 1573; indeed he could hardly have avoided exposure to it in one manner or another.

Whether or not Sidney in the early 1570s accepted the humanist glorification of Venice, he had clearly come to reject it by the time he wrote to his brother Robert from England in May 1578. As one of a number of travel suggestions, he singled out Venice from other Italian cities for its "good lawes, & customs." But then, reversing himself, he warned instantly that these "wee can hardly proporcion to our selves, because they [i.e., the Venetians] are quite of a contrary government, there is little there but tyranous oppression, & servile yeilding to them, that have little or no rule over them" (3:127). Sidney's 1578 condemnation of another traditional exemplum of the mixed state reflects, I believe, the influence of Jean Bodin's *Republic* (1576). Bodin attacks the Venetian humanists such as Contarini and Giannotti for claiming that Venice is a mixed state because, he claims, it turns out that the Venetian "mixture" is weighted heavily in favor of the aristocratic Senate and against the monarchic Doge, who constitutes but a "fictitious image" of a king. Since according to Bodin sovereignty is indivisible, always residing with one element or another of the putative mixture, in the case of Venice it must be said to reside with the aristocrats, and therefore Venice, for all its reputation as a mixed state, is an aristocracy pure and simple. Its populace suffers accordingly.[19] This discussion is cognate with Bodin's aforementioned critique of the Spartan myth. In both cases, he claims, the true historical condition belies the humanist myth of equilibrium.

Whether or not Sidney's analysis of either state derives from Bodin, his external critique of the Venetian myth coordinates precisely with his internal, or fictional, critique of the Spartan myth. In both cases Sidney not only suggests that republican models are inapplicable to such a centralized monarchy as England—noting in the 1578 letter that "wee can hardly proporcion" Venice to ourselves, and noting in the 1580 fiction that classical republicanism constitutes "a matter more in imaginacion than practice"—but also goes on to make the more radical claim that such models are inherently unstable. As he claims in the 1578 letter that there is little in Venice but "tyranous oppression, & servile yeilding to them, that have little or noe rule over them," by which he evidently means that the Venetian *grandi* oppress the subservient *popolo*, so in *New Arcadia* he represents Sparta as riven by the class warfare of gentlemen against Helots. In both cases the republican polities suffer by contrast with monarchy, the 1578 letter implicitly poising Venetian inequity against English stability and the *New Arcadia* measuring the "wasted soile" of Sparta against the "delightfull prospects" of monarchic Arcadia. Both internal and external texts thus suggest that the class warfare of nobles against commoners results directly from a charac-

[19]Jean Bodin, *La République* 2.1, cf. 2.7.

teristic feature of republican models—the depressed kingship, whether the incapacitated Doge or the feeble Spartan monarchs.

Further, both texts acquire definition in the light of Jean Bodin's critique of the central theme of republicanism, divided or mixed sovereignty, and of his censure of the great republican exemplars, Venice and Sparta. I consider nothing more likely than that Bodin influenced Sidney, for both of his other two "mates in song," Fulke Greville and Edward Dyer, studied Bodin's *Republic*, and so much in *Arcadia* apart from the critique of Sparta is compatible with a Bodinian outlook that one hardly knows where to begin suggesting specific parallels.[20] Let me simply suggest for now that both Bodin and Sidney share the same advocacy of a highly centralized monarchy and the same suspicion of the federalist, noble-oriented doctrine of the monarchomachs.

I hesitate, however, to credit Sidney's thought exclusively to Bodin. For one thing this would obscure the originality of his own Spartan episode, one that may owe as much to the minority report of antiquity as to Bodin. While I feel that Bodin's critique of the mixed state in general must have guided Sidney, in the particular case of Sparta the poet's analysis may be more radical, better grounded in the true historical problem of that ancient state: it is he rather than Bodin who draws attention to the tragedy of the Helots, a tragedy that continues to intrigue modern historians.[21] Secondly, to refer Sidney's critique exclusively to Bodin would obscure the fact that it is a fictional and dramatic one, which is to say that it entertains the republican assumptions and terms even if ultimately to discredit them.

This chapter has discussed Sidney's appraisal of the classical political idiom generally rather than the monarchomachs specifically. Nevertheless it impinges on Sidney's attitude toward the monarchomachs in several ways. First, these were among the most salient

---

[20]For Bodin's influence on Fulke Greville, cf. Hugh MacLean, "Kingship and Sovereignty," *HLQ* 16 (1952–1953), 237–271; for Bodin and Edward Dyer, cf. R. M. Sargent, *The Life and Lyrics of Edward Dyer* (Oxford: Clarendon Press, 1968), p. 49. Sidney's slighting reference to Bodin's earlier *Method for the Easy Comprehension of History* (3:130) should not be taken as indicating his disapproval of the far more original *Republic*. His sympathy with Bodinian themes has been generally overlooked. Allan Gilbert presented an unpublished paper on this subject in the 1930s; it is mentioned in Goldman, pp. 184–185.

[21]Of modern historians writing on this topic, I will mention P. Oliva, *Sparta and Her Social Problems* (Amsterdam: A. Hakkert, 1971).

contemporary champions of this idiom, drawing indiscriminately
on classical terms and models without pausing to reflect whether
such models were indeed fully applicable to the "present case" of
sixteenth century monarchy. Second, the monarchomachs shared
with the classical masters a profoundly aristocratic bias. All men of
noble stock and retainers of noblemen, they looked upon the common man with disdain, repeatedly reserving rebellion as an aristocratic privilege.[22] While their generally aristocratic sympathies do
not distinguish them from Sidney, their unfortunate tendency to
regard the submission of commoner to nobleman as ordained by
nature does. Sidney's conception of political order, as we shall see,
was more pragmatic and expeditious than that of his French
friends, and he does not seem to have possessed their confidence in
generalizing from social accident to hierarchical reason. Thirdly,
Sidney's Spartan wars may be said to act out one of the internal
contradictions with which monarchomach theory is rife: for while
these theorists utilized a myth of original freedom for the purpose
of their own class, they would no doubt have considered indecent
the mobilization of such an argument by Helots.

Sidney never directly dismisses the libertarian party as do its absolutist opponents including Jean Bodin, its most formidable and
penetrating one. Rather he extends to the reader of *Arcadia* an
invitation to consider the results of its cardinal ideas. Let us consider such theories as that of the subaltern magistrate and that of
classical republicanism not in the abstract but consequentially: let us
test them dramatically and see where they take us. No less crucial to
this procedure than the final conclusion is the original invitation.
For we must begin by taking these ideas seriously if we are to feel the
loss involved in their rejection. Thus Amphialus must seem attractive; Musidorus must be washed ashore onto Sparta and Pyrocles
come to the aid of its helotry; the justifications of sundry revolting
parties must, echoing "true commonplaces," seem sententious and
plausible; and the most crucial Arcadian text of all must be delivered
by someone named "old Languet" and must appeal to us as a confirmation of the *Vindiciae contra tyrannos*.

---

[22]Cf. Beza, *Du droit des magistrats*, pp. 8, 53, 75; also Languet, pp. 109–112, 213.

CHAPTER FOUR

Give Us A King

Philisides' Fable I

The Jews well know their pow'r: ere Saul they chose,
God was their king, and God they durst depose.—Dryden

[1]

WHILE THE TWO PREVIOUS CHAPTERS HAVE DISCUSSED INCIDENTS in
the *New Arcadia,* this and the next turn to a text in the *Old
Arcadia* that already fully enunciates Sidney's critique of the monarchomachs. Indeed nowhere does Sidney engage the monarchomachs more directly and personally than in the "Ister banke"
eclogue: whereas Amphialus' rebellion focuses on a single aspect of
monarchomach thought, the subaltern magistrate, and whereas the
Spartan wars focus less on the monarchomachs than on the classical
republicanism of which they comprise but a contemporary illustration, "Ister banke" focusses directly on Sidney's Polonius, Hubert
Languet, and on Languet's *Vindiciae,* the most notorious of the
monarchomach works. It focusses on Languet's doctrine in order to
reject it decisively. But no text better illustrates the cost to the poet of
such a rejection.

Between each "Book or Act" of *Arcadia* occurs material of a
pastoral nature serving as interlude or *entr'acte.* As part of the Third
Eclogues of *Old Arcadia,* a young shepherd named Philisides recites
a beast-fable in the rhyme royal stanza. Philisides is generally considered Sidney's "fictionalized self-portrait"[1] on the grounds (a)
that his name recalls the poet's in two ways, "Philisides" conflating

---

[1]William A. Ringler, Jr. (ed.), *The Poems of Sir Philip Sidney* (Oxford: Clarendon
Press, 1962), p. 418.

the first syllables of the name *Phil*ip *Sid*ney and, as "lover of a star" *(phili + sidus),* comprising the etymologic equivalent of Sidney's other great *persona,* Astrophil; (b) that Philisides elsewhere delivers a personal history approximating Sidney's own (4:312-13); and (c) that the present text refers to an actual event in Sidney's biography.

This poem's date of composition is germane. We don't know when Sidney began the *Old Arcadia*—Molyneaux reported that it dates from 1577—but we do know that much of it belongs to 1580, when Sidney spent several months at Wilton: the poet told his brother Robert in October 1580 that he would have Philip's "toyfull booke" by the following February (3:132), and one of the old *Old Arcadia* manuscripts is dated 1580.[2] In any event, a happy accident enables us to date the particular text in question to 1579-1580. This is its use of an archaic diction obviously inspired by Edmund Spenser's *Shepherd's Calendar* (i.e., such words as couthe, for to bene, heard, mickle, ne, n'is, reed, stowers, swincke, thilke, tho, welkin, won'd). The *Calendar,* which was dedicated to Sidney, was entered in the Stationer's Register on December 1, 1579. Either Sidney wrote his Spenser imitations, of which "Ister banke" is one of several in the *Old Arcadia,* in 1579 prior to the publication of the *Calendar* when both he and Spenser were resident at Leicester House and he held Spenser "in some use of familiarity";[3] or else Sidney wrote these imitations in 1580, perhaps after retiring to Wilton in March, when the *Calendar* existed in published form.[4] While I prefer the latter date on the ground that the myth of an English "Areopagus" involving these two poets' composing in proximity no longer commands general assent, either date would serve my purpose.

Fifteen-eighty, then: during the previous autumn, Hubert Languet had published the first edition of his *Vindiciae contra tyrannos,* and would publish the second in the course of this year. This fact is germane because Sidney's text refers to Languet in two different ways: it refers quite explicitly to his name, and then it refers implicitly (so several readers have felt) to his doctrine. When Sidney was writing, this doctrine had just been publicly and notoriously (if

---

[2]This is the Phillips MS, for a description of which see Ringler or Jean Robertson (ed.), *The Countess of Pembroke's Arcadia (The Old Arcadia)* (Oxford: Clarendon Press, 1973).

[3]As Spenser reported in a letter to Gabriel Harvey dated 5 Oct. 1579; cf. R. E. Neil Dodge (ed.), *The Complete Poetical Works of Spenser* (Boston: Houghton Mifflin, 1908), p. 769.

[4]Robertson, p. xix, prefers the former alternative.

pseudonymously) expounded; and indeed Sidney's text constitutes
the earliest reasoned response to the *Vindiciae* of which I am aware
(see Appendix A).

The explicit reference to Languet every reader of Sidney knows.
In the "frame" stanzas preceding the fable proper, Philisides ascribes the fable to "Languet, the shepheard best swift Ister knewe"
(the Ister, or Danube, flows through Vienna, Languet's base of op-
erations for much of the 1570s). Anyone, however, who wishes to
argue Sidney's sympathy with "old Languet" takes upon himself the
task of explaining why the poet was not more responsive to Languet
at the very time he wrote his famous lines of praise, inevitably
quoted in the biographies as proof of Sidney's devotion:

> The songe I sange old Languet had me taught,
> Languet, the shepheard best swift Ister knewe,
> For clerkly reed, and hating what is naught,
> For faithfull hart, cleane hands, and mouth as true: [25]
> With his sweet skill my skillesse youth he drewe,
>   To have a feeling tast of him that sitts
>   Beyond the heaven, far more beyond your witts.

> He said, the Musique best thilke powers pleasd
> Was jumpe concorde between our wit and will: [30]
> Where highest notes to godlines are raisd,
> And lowest sink not downe to jote of ill:
> With old true tales he woont mine eares to fill,
>   Howe sheepheards did of yore, how now they thrive,
>   Spoiling their flock, or while twixt them they strive.   [35]

> He liked me, but pitied lustfull youth:
> His good strong staffe my slippry yeares upbore:
> He still hop'd well, because I loved truth;
> Till forste to parte, with harte and eyes even sore,
> To worthy Coredens he gave me ore.   [40]
>   But thus in oke's true shade recounted he
>   Which now in night's deepe shade sheep heard of me.[5]

[5]The lineation is Ringler's. These stanzas are quoted as proof of Sidney's indebted-
ness to Languet by Thomas Zouch, *Memoirs of the Life and Writings of Sir Philip Sidney*
(2nd ed.; York, 1809), p. 57; Sarah M. Davis, *The Life and Times of Sir Philip Sidney*
(Boston: Ticknor and Fields, 1859), p. 69; H. R. Fox Bourne, *Sir Philip Sidney: Type of
Chivalry in the Elizabethan Age* (New York: E. P. Putnam, 1891), pp. 67–68; J. A.
Symonds, *Sir Philip Sidney* (London: Macmillan, 1909), pp. 103–104; W. A. Bradley
(ed.), *The Correspondence of Philip Sidney and Hubert Languet* (Boston: Merrymount
Press, 1912), pp. xxxi-xxxii; E. M. Denkinger, *Immortal Sidney* (New York: Brentano's,

For at the very time that Sidney was writing these lines, he was also responding to Languet's exhortation to join him—to join, that is to say, the Protestant resistance—with a definitive "no." The principal theme of the correspondence between Sidney and Languet during 1580 is the question of the active, engaged life versus the contemplative. Languet could not begin to understand why Sidney did not commit himself frankly and immediately to the activist bloc on the continent. Why, of all times, retire now, at the moment when the activist machine centered on William of Orange was moving into high gear, given Languet's publication of a theory of resistance at the suggestion of Loyseleur de Villiers, William's chaplain; given the finalization of François d'Anjou's sovereignty of Flanders and Brabant (secretly mediated for Orange by Languet in May 1580); and given Orange's own impending *Protestation* against the Spanish tyranny (November 1580)? But as often as Languet wrote to Sidney during this year urging him to embrace the moment, so often did Sidney demur.[6] The poet compounded this demurral by choosing this moment to commit himself to fiction—an act that from the perspective of Languet's functionalist mentality was nothing short of frivolous.

It isn't entirely clear why Sidney was reluctant to cross the channel in 1580. Perhaps the activist design was rendered chancy for him by Orange and Languet's insistence on including François d'Anjou in their plans; as we have seen, Sidney had excoriated Anjou in 1579 for "thrusting himself in the low country matters" (though Sidney's skepticism as to the Valois prince would await 1584 and the *New Arcadia* for its fictional enunciation, by which time everyone realized what Anjou had been about). Whatever the reason for Sidney's refusal to budge (and it may be misleading to isolate the Anjou question, since Sidney's skepticism may have addressed the cause rather than any one actor), the fact is that he did refuse at precisely the moment he penned his lines in praise of Languet.

1931), pp. 212–213; Marcus Goldman, *Sir Philip Sidney and the Arcadia* (Urbana: University of Illinois Press, 1934), p. 176; Alfred H. Bill, *Astrophel: Or the Life and Death of the Renowned Sir Philip Sidney* (London: Cassell, 1938), pp. 118–119; Ringler, pp. xxi–xxii; Geoffrey Shepherd in his introduction to Sidney's *Apology for Poetry* (London: Nelson, 1965), p. 6; and Roger Howell, *Sir Philip Sidney: The Shepherd Knight* (London: Hutchinson, 1968), pp. 151–152. Robertson, Sidney's latest editor (p. 463), terms the fable "Sidney's tribute to Hubert Languet."

    [6]Cf. Languet to Sidney on January 30, March 12, May 6, September 24, and October 22, 1580.

This does not mean that the frame stanzas in praise of Languet are devoid of meaning. At the very least they have an autobiographical reference since they inform us that Languet was wont to fill a young man's ears "with old true tales"

> How sheepheards did of yore, how now they thrive,
> Spoiling their flock, or while twixt them they strive

—a biographical fact that I shall argue is painstakingly accurate. Whether or not Sidney listened to these "old true tales," however, is another question entirely.

I said that Sidney's text refers to Languet in two different ways. While the frame stanzas refer explicitly to his person, the fable itself, the text of which follows, may be said to refer implicitly to his doctrine:

> Such maner time there was (what time I n'ot)
> When all this Earth, this damme or mould of ours,
> Was onely won'd with such as beastes begot: [45]
> Unknowne as then were they that buylden towers:
> The cattell wild, or tame, in nature's bowers
>   Might freely rome, or rest, as seemed them:
>   Man was not man their dwellings in to hem.

> The beastes had sure some beastly pollicie: [50]
> For nothing can endure where order n'is.
> For once the Lion by the Lambe did lie;
> The fearefull Hinde the Leoparde did kisse:
> Hurtles was Tyger's pawe and Serpent's hisse.
>   This thinke I well, the beasts with courage clad   [55]
>   Like Senators a harmeles empire had.

> At which, whether the others did repine,
> (For envie harbreth most in feeblest hartes)
> Or that they all to chaunging did encline,
> (As even in beasts their dammes leave chaunging parts)   [60]
> The multitude to *Jove* a suite empartes,
>   With neighing, blaying, braying, and barking,
>   Roring, and howling for to have a King.

> A King, in language theirs they said they would:
> (For then their language was a perfect speech)
> The birdes likewise with chirpes, and puing could,   [65]
> Cackling, and chattring, that of *Jove* beseech.

Onely the owle still warnde them not to seech
So hastily that which they would repent:
But sawe they would, and he to deserts went.   [70]

Jove wisely said (for wisdome wisely sayes)
'O beasts, take heed what you of me desire.
Rulers will thinke all things made them to please,
And soone forget the swincke due to their hire.
But since you will, part of my heav'nly fire   [75]
  I will you lende; the rest your selves must give,
  That it both seene and felte may with you live.'

Full glad they were and tooke the naked sprite,
Which streight the Earth yclothed in his claye:
The Lion, harte; the Ounce gave active might;   [80]
The Horse, good shape; the Sparrow, lust to playe;
Nightingale, voice, entising songes to saye.
  Elephant gave a perfect memorie:
  And Parot, ready tongue, that to applie.

The Foxe gave crafte; the Dog gave flatterie;   [85]
Asse, pacience; the Mole, a working thought;
Eagle, high looke; Wolfe secrete crueltie:
Monkie, sweet breath; the Cow, her faire eyes brought;
The Ermion, whitest skinne, spotted with nought;
  The sheepe, mild-seeing face; climing, the Beare;   [90]
  The Stagge did give the harme eschewing feare.

The Hare, her sleights; the Cat, his melancholie;
Ante, industrie; and Connie, skill to builde;
Cranes, order; Storkes, to be appearing holie;
Camaeleon, ease to chaunge; Ducke, ease to yelde;   [95]
Crocodile, teares, which might be falsely spilde;
  Ape great thing gave, though he did moving[7] stand,
  The instrument of instruments, the hand.

Ech other beast likewise his present brings:
And (but they drad their Prince they ofte should want)   [100]

[7]Here is my only departure from the texts of Ringler and Robertson. I prefer a
well-attested variant, "moving," to their "mowing," which is nonsense. The meaning
of the couplet is this: by walking erect ("moving stand"), the ape freed his hands to
become graspers of tools (i.e., "instruments of instruments"). This interpretation
requires that "though" in the subordinate clause have the value of "since" (*since* he
stood, he freed his hands), a usage that, while unusual, has Elizabethan precedent; cf.
Love's Labor's Lost 2.1.221: "My lips are no common, though several they be."

They all consented were to give him wings:
And aye more awe towards him for to plant,
To their owne worke this priviledge they graunt,
  That from thenceforth to all eternitie,
  No beast should freely speake, but onely he.   [105]

Thus Man was made; thus Man their Lord became:
Who at the first, wanting, or hiding pride,
He did to beastes' best use his cunning frame;
With water drinke, herbes meate, and naked hide,
And fellow-like let his dominion slide;   [110]
  Not in his sayings saying I, but we:
  As if he meant his lordship common be.

But when his seate so rooted he had found,
That they now skilld not, how from him to wend;
Then gan in guiltlesse earth full many a wound,   [115]
Iron to seeke, which gainst it selfe should bend,
To teare the bowels, that good corne should send.
  But yet the common Damme none did bemone;
  Because (though hurt) they never heard her grone.

Then gan he factions in the beastes to breed;   [120]
Where helping weaker sort, the nobler beastes,
(As Tygers, leopards, beares, and Lions' seed)
Disdaind with this, in deserts sought their restes;
Where famine ravine taught their hungrie chestes,
  That craftily he forst them to do ill,   [125]
  Which being done he afterwards would kill.

For murdre done, which never erst was seene,
By those great beastes, as for the weaker's good,
He chose themselves his guarders for to bene,
Gainst those of might, of whom in feare they stood,   [130]
As horse and dogge, not great, but gentle blood:
  Blithe were the commons, cattell of the fielde,
  Tho when they saw their foen of greatness kilde.

But they or spent, or made of slender might,
Then quickly did the meaner cattell finde,   [135]
The great beames gone, the house on shoulders light:
For by and by the horse faire bitts did binde:
The dogge was in a coller taught his kinde.
  As for the gentle birds, like case might rewe,
  When falcon they, and gossehauke saw in mewe.   [140]

Worst fell to smallest birds, and meanest heard,
Who now his owne, full like his owne he used.
Yet first but wooll, or fethers off he teard:
And when they were well us'de to be abused,
For hungrie throte their flesh with teeth he brused: [145]
    At length for glutton taste he did them kill:
    At last for sport their sillie lives did spill.

But yet ô man, rage not beyond thy neede:
Deeme it no gloire to swell in tyrannie.
Thou art of blood; joy not to make things bleede: [150]
Thou fearest death; thinke they are loth to die.
A plaint of guiltlesse hurt doth pierce the skie.
    And you poore beasts, in patience bide your hell,
    Or know your strengths, and then you shall do well.

To paraphrase: once upon a time the community of animals lived
an Edenic life (ll. 43-56). Then, whether the common beasts re-
sented the empire of those "with courage clad" or because the entire
community "to chaunging did encline," the beasts demanded of
Jove a king. Though warned by the owl that they would repent their
demand, the beasts persevered, and a reluctant Jove finally agreed
to create a king as their ruler, a king compounded partly of their
animal attributes and partly of his own "heav'nly fire"—in short,
Man (ll. 57-105). Although at first this king ruled equitably, he soon
began to breed factionalism among the beasts, first siding with the
weaker beasts against the nobler and then, upon the elimination of
the nobler, turning upon the weaker as well, so that eventually he
secured dominion over the entire animal kingdom (ll. 106-47). To
this fable as such, Philisides appends one stanza of *moralitas* (ll.
148-54). This much of the text constitutes what the shepherd
Philisides sang to his original audience—his flock of sheep—upon a
certain occasion; seven "frame" stanzas, six preceding and one following (ll. 1-42, 155-61), allow Philisides to clarify the dramatic
context of that earlier occasion for his present audience—the crew
of Arcadian shepherds—and to explain the fable's provenance from
"old Languet" and praise its author.

As to sources, the fable as such is original with Sidney. It makes
certain allusions to traditional material: the prelapsarian condition
of *integritas*—"For once the Lion by the Lambe did lie"—echoes
Isaiah as well as Ovid's description of the Golden Age; the demand
for a king recalls 1 Samuel 8; the confection of Man from the differ-

ent qualities of beasts comes from the Prometheus myth; the archaic diction is Spenserian; and the genre Sidney is working here, that of the beast fable, is a venerable one (its use may also have been suggested to Sidney by the *Shepherd's Calendar,* which has a couple of examples in the genre).[8] The total configuration of the fable, however, is unique to Sidney. Whatever its political import, the poetic and fabulous elements at least surely cannot—with due respect to Philisides—derive from Hubert Languet since he never wrote a line of poetry in his life, and on the strength of their three treatises it is safe to say that he and the other monarchomachs were rarely tempted by metaphor.[9]

[2]

On the other hand, Sidney has contrived to make it easy for us to perceive in his fable an allusion to political ideas publicized by Languet and other "king-fighters." Clearly the fable has something to do with the problem of tyranny, and to raise this subject in 1580 was to invoke such works as the *Vindiciae* and the *De jure regni.* Most students of the fable, then—who happen to be far fewer in number than the biographers who quote the stanzas of praise framing it— have been able to conclude that its teachings are congruent with those of Languet.[10]

[8]Ringler, p. 414, also adduces the Aesopic fable about frogs who ask for a king, but I don't think this bears directly on our poem.

[9]The monarchomachs wrote very little "poetry" in the Sidnean sense, that is, secular fiction. Beza and Buchanan composed plays on scriptural subject matter, and Beza collaborated in a metaphrase of the psalms and—the exception—wrote some notorious poems, mostly juvenalia, on lyrical-amatory topics. So far as I know, Hotman and Languet wrote neither verse nor fiction of any sort.

[10]Cf. Ringler, p. 413, and Robertson, p. 464, as well as: Martin Bergbusch, "Political Thought and Conduct in Sidney's *Arcadia*" (Ph.D. dissertation, Cornell University, 1971), pp. 13–15, 50–56, 121–123, 154, 232–235; Martin Bergbusch, "Rebellion in the *New Arcadia,*" *PQ* 53 (1974), 29–41; W. D. Briggs, "Political Ideas in Sidney's *Arcadia,*" *SP* 28 (1931), 137–61; W. D. Briggs, "Sidney's Political Ideas," *SP* 29 (1932), 534–542; Norman Levine, "Aspects of Moral and Political Thought in Sidney's *Arcadia*" (Ph.D. dissertation, Columbia University, 1972), pp. 12–20; C. S. Levy, "The Correspondence of Sir Philip Sidney and Hubert Languet 1572–76" (Ph.D. dissertation, Cornell 1962), pp. xlix–l; and E. W. Talbert, *The Problem of Order: Elizabethan Political Commonplaces and an Example of Shakespeare's Art* (Chapel Hill: University of North Carolina Press, 1962), pp. 97–99. However, Irving Ribner in "Sir Philip Sidney on Civil Insurrection," *JHI* 13 (1952), anticipates my view. The theories of Ephim Fogel and J. A. van Dorsten, according to which the fable constitutes a topical allegory pertaining to the year 1579, are dealt with later.

Indeed, our text might be set to represent a translation into fable of a long setpiece from Question Three of the *Vindiciae* which recapitulates the traditional attributes of the evil ruler and more specifically of the "tyrant by conduct":

> Since a tyrant is the opposite of a king, it follows either that he has seized authority by force or fraud [the "tyrant without title"], or that he is a king who rules a kingdom freely given him in a manner contrary to equity and justice and persists in that misrule in violation of the laws and compacts to which he took a solemn oath [the "tyrant by conduct"].

> A tyrant lops off those ears which grow higher than the rest of the corn, especially where virtue makes them most conspicuously eminent; oppresses by calumnies and fraudulent practices the principal officers of the state; gives out reports of intended conspiracies against himself, that he might have some colourable pretext to cut them off . . . advances above and in opposition to the ancient and worthy nobility, mean and unworthy persons . . . hates and suspects discreet and wise men, and fears no opposition more than virtue. . . . A tyrant nourishes and feeds factions and dissentions amongst his subjects, ruins one by the help of another, that he may the easier vanquish the remainder. . . . A tyrant leaves no design unattempted by which he may fleece his subjects of their substance, and turn it to his proper benefit, that being continually troubled in gaining means to live, they may have no leisure, no hope, how to regain their liberty.[11]

The actions of the ruler depicted in the fable would seem to tally with this traditional portrait of the *tyrannus exercitio*, for example, as regards his "nourish[ing] and feed[ing] factions and dissentions amongst his subjects, ruin[ing] one by the help of another, that he may the easier vanquish the remainder," his suppression of the nobility in particular, and his diversion of community resources to his own pleasure: compare 11. 112-47 of the fable, which describe Man's breeding factionalism between the nobler beasts and the weaker, the entire collapse of the animal kingdom following his elimination of the nobility, and his plunder of his own subjects to the point of killing them "for glutton taste" and at last and most cruelly

---

[11]See Hubert Languet, *A Defense of Liberty Against Tyrants* (1924; reprinted, Gloucester, Mass.: Peter Smith, 1963), pp. 183ff. For the first paragraph, however, I prefer the modern translation by Julian H. Franklin (trans. and ed.), *Constitutionalism and Resistance in the Sixteenth Century* (New York: Pegasus, 1969), p. 185.

"for sport." Indeed at the conclusion of his fable, Philisides does not hesitate to put the obvious label on Man's actions: "Deem it no gloire," he warns Man in the appended *moralitas*, "to swell *in tyrannie*" (1. 148).

The final situation in the fable, then, with the community's subserving the ruler's pleasure, seems unambiguously vicious. It has seemed obvious to most readers that, since the fable describes a transition from law to tyranny, its lesson must be that the tyrant should be brought to account or placed under constitutional supervision. This can be done, most exegetes have suggested, by reinstating something of the order that obtained before the accession of the monarch-tyrant, that is, by rehabilitating the powerful or "nobler" beasts and providing them with such constitutional authority as Languet and the other monarchomachs insist should be invested in the nobility. Thus William A. Ringler, the editor of Sidney's poems: "Whatever the specific reference, the general moral is clear—a powerful aristocracy is the best safeguard of the common people against tyranny."[12] Just as the monarchomachs would reverse the trend of the century by returning sovereignty to those feudal nobles ruthlessly suppressed by the advent of centralized monarchy, so our fable would mitigate the sovereignty of tyrant Man by returning a share of it to those "nobler beastes" whom he had been particularly anxious to eliminate. This is Languet, with the investiture simply of rhyme royal; and Philisides' introductory lines of praise are no more than a happy nod in the direction of the fable's only begetter.

[3]

That the doctrine of the fable alludes to Hubert Languet's, I have no doubt. In adducing the *Vindiciae*, the critics have done no more than follow the directions of the poet, who provides us with a suitably blood-drenched "tyrant by conduct" and, in case we miss the point, flies Languet's name over the whole performance—we couldn't have asked anything more of Sidney in the way of cues, and I for one am happy to begin by looking in the direction to which they point.

Yet there are a number of discrepancies between our fable and the monarchomach position. They concern less Sidney's characteri-

[12]Ringler, p. 413.

zation of the ruler's manner of making free with his subjects' "goods"
and lives—for such conduct the only suitable name is tyrannic, as
Philisides recognizes—than the moral to be drawn, the posture to be
assumed, once the fact of the tyrant is given. To find the moral, we
go to the stanza of *moralitas* which Philisides appends to the action.
Of the seven lines of the rhyme royal stanza, Philisides addresses five
to the ruler and two to the subjects. The five lines addressed to
Man—

> But yet ô man, rage not beyond thy neede:
> Deeme it no gloire to swell in tyrannie.
> Thou art of blood; joy not to make things bleede:
> Thou fearest death; thinke they are loth to die.
> A plaint of guiltlesse hurt doth pierce the skie (ll. 148-52)

—clearly pass a kind of ethical judgment on Man's behavior; but it is
hard to discover any specifically political posture here beyond the
tone of reprobation; what the last line suggests—that the cries of the
innocent subject-victims will "pierce the skie," that is, reach God
(who will then presumably cause the tyrant to be punished)—does
not resemble the monarchomach attitude to tyrants insofar as it
slides into the traditional inscrutability (let God handle it) rather
than gearing for action.

As for the two lines addressed to the suffering beasts, they make
precisely the suggestion that the monarchomachs devoted themselves to combating:

> And you poore beastes, in patience bide your hell

Patience! This too was the traditional sop thrown to the community
in the clutches of a tyrant—the traditional Christian consolation. We
find it in Augustine, in Calvin, in innumerable homilies, in just
about everybody in the sixteenth century except the monarchomachs and a few other parties. Whatever this is, it is certainly not
Languet's attitude; it is not the attitude of the "king-fighters," who
argued that the community must rise up against the tyrant, not
tolerate him, not "bide [its] hell," not defer to some inscrutably
divine historical dialectic for the evening up of accounts. As a
pseudonym under which to publish the *Vindiciae* Languet took no
less polemical a name than that of Junius Brutus, who forcibly ended

the tyranny of the Tarquin kings. The moral of Philisides' story for
the monarchomachs would be not patience, but tyrannicide.

It is true that another line follows, one that has been taken to
concur with Languet's outlook:

> . . . in patience bide your hell,
> Or know your strengths, and then you shall do well.

On this line advocates of a monarchomach Sidney regularly pitch
their case. If we identify the beasts' "strengths" as the various gifts
they originally donated to the personality of the monarch, for
example, "harte," "active might," "good shape," and so on, then this
line may mean: Act purposively so as to reclaim something of your
antique prerogatives.[13] Or perhaps "strengths" refers to those aristocrats suppressed by the tyrant; thus according to Ringler this line
exhorts the community to "be aware that the aristocrats are the
protectors of the commons against tyranny."[14] However, these radical constructions seem undercut by the nature of the imperative
involved, which is not a verb of action but the verb "know," suggesting a solution in acquiescence in a given state of affairs rather than
confrontation or action. There is actually a whole spectrum of possibilities for this line, depending on what we make of that enigmatic
counsel to "know your strengths," ranging from the aforementioned radical constructions to Ribner's "be aware that your strength
is in God, not in political action,"[15] a reading that would tally with
the orientation of the victims' "plaint" to the "skie" (1. 152). Whatever the meaning of this, the second line of the couplet addressed to
the beasts, the first line of the couplet isn't ambiguous at all and
announces a posture toward the problem of the tyrant that is
diametrically opposed to that of the monarchomachs.

In claiming, then, that *since* the fable describes the accession of a
tyrant, *then* its lesson should be that he must immediately be brought
to account or placed under constitutional control, the critics may
have made an unwarranted leap. That the ruler acts tyrannically
does not necessarily mean that Sidney is calling for his chastisement.
Philisides does not call for the tyrant to be chastised by any agency

[13]I paraphrase Bergbusch, "Political Thought and Conduct," pp. 52, 232–235.
[14]Ringler, p. 414.
[15]Ribner, 260–261.

external to himself; he simply asks the tyrant not to "rage . . . beyond
his neede" (whatever that may be), not to consider such raging
"gloire," not to *enjoy* making things bleed, not to deny his victims his
own fear of death (11.148-51)—he asks all of these things, but conspicuously he does not ask Man to refrain from having his way with
his subjects. The point is rather that he should not put the wrong
name on his behavior, call it "gloire," say, when it is something else.

Thus our fable generally poses the *problem* of the tyrant rather
than any solutions. It poses this problem as sensationally as any of
the monarchomachs, and Sidney's portrait of a ruler so enthusiasti-
cally shedding his subjects' blood surely owes something to the activist literature of the 1570s. For the monarchomachs, the problem
of the tyrant was only the starting point, the given: they have a place
in political theory because of the activist solutions they proposed.
Just where the monarchomachs, however, begin to talk of epho-
rates, parliaments, estates, diets, and officers of the crown, Sidney's
fable is conspicuously silent. Of its 161 lines, only one, and that a
cryptic one, suggests anything like the aggressive posture of the
monarchomachs—if it suggests that at all. Turning from this text to
Arcadia at large, we can look all day up and down in the 900-some
pages of this fiction without coming across more than a few small
hints of the king-fighters' constitutional machinery—the ephorate
and parliaments and so on—or, as we have seen in previous chapters,
any reminiscences of the king-fighters' idiom and arguments are
carefully enclosed within an ironic context. "In patience bide your
hell": if this is the moral of the story, then something, or someone,
has intervened between Hubert Languet and our text.

                                    [4]

By adducing the traditional articles of Golden Age lore both biblical and classical, Philisides evidently represents the "beastlie pollicie" as idyllic, and the tyrant's perversion of that polity as pre-
cipitating the Iron Age. (Thus, for only a partial list, 1. 46, "Unknowne as then were they that buylden towers," alludes to the
period prior to the accession of Nimrod, the first tyrant; 11. 47-48
recall Ovid's description of the Golden Age when men had no fixed
dwellings, cf. *Metam.* 1.89-112; 11. 52-54 utilize Isaiah's millenarian
vision; conversely ll. 115-19, when Man "gan in guiltlesse earth . . .

Iron to seek," echo the commonplace that mining for metals is symptomatic of postlapsarian life, cf. *Metam.* 1.137-40.) That Sidney represents the monarch's securing of dominion over his subjects in terms of a lapse from *integritas* does not necessarily mean, however, that he is arguing for a return to the lapsed or eclipsed condition; indeed his fable omits any explicit call for such a return. Further, while the Gold versus Iron scheme suggests a prima facie compatibility with a characteristic libertarian attitude, Sidney develops that scheme in a way that is finally quite antithetical to the monarchomachs.

The myth of an original, once-upon-a-time freedom from the depredations of tyrants plays a central role in the thought of the king-fighters; indeed, as Walzer notes wittily, "the myth of origins has, so far as modern times are concerned, its origin here."[16] Hotman's *Francogallia* gives currency to this myth, claiming that the first French kings were creatures of communal decision. The other monarchomachs follow suit, discovering ancient, Edenic constitutions under the accretions of their countries' history.[17] Let us, urges the author of the *Reveille-Matin*, "ramener l'estat à son principe" — return the state to its original, which is to say its natural, condition.[18] However, while the monarchomachs share with our fable a nostalgia for "Such maner time," their Eden is not Philisides'.

The polity Philisides depicts in Edenic terms is clearly something along the lines of an aristocracy since the "nobler" beasts such as "Tygers, leopards, beares, and Lions' seed" rule over the "weaker," such as horses, dogs, cattle, and birds. Now in one respect this recalls a monarchomach tendency because, as we have had occasion to see in earlier chapters, a characteristic feature of these thinkers is their desire to reinvigorate the feudal nobility. But in one crucial respect the Edenic "beastlie pollicie" does not correspond to the monarchomach ideal at all. The ideal of the monarchomachs is never aristocracy pure and simple but rather constitutional, strictly limited monarchy. It is true that they place a great deal of emphasis on the "great nobles of the kingdom" (*regni proceres*) or on an aristocratic senate or estates as limiting agencies on the king. But monarchy

---

[16]Michael Walzer, *The Revolution of the Saints* (New York: Atheneum, 1973), p. 76.

[17]Buchanan does this for Scotland in *Rerum scoticarum historia* (1582); in the *Apology of William of Orange* (1581) the authors, probably Languet and Marnix, elaborate a Burgundian myth of origins for the Low Countries.

[18]*Reveille-Matin des français et de leurs voisins* (1574) 2:116.

itself never drops out of the picture; the king always constitutes one element in a "mixed state." Thus for Hotman, the Golden Age of French history, the "antiquum et tanquam naturalem statum,"[19] is a period not of aristocracy but rather of elective monarchy. In fact, the ideal of Languet's *Vindiciae* is actually a form of hereditary monarchy since the people have the right to elect as their king not any individual but only one within the royal blood or "race" (thus the crucial role of François d'Anjou, a Valois, in Languet's plans). Similarly, Beza argues for a constitutional kingship that while "électif quant à la personne" remains "succesif quant à la race."[20]

We can thus approach the fable as a study in some of the confusions to which the myth of origins lends itself. For when we apply to the fable the radical injunction to "ramener l'estat à son principe" —and the Golden Age echoes encourage precisely this reflex—we find ourselves excavating a political stratum that is too primitive even for the monarchomachs. To return "au principe" in Sidney's fable is to arrive at pure aristocracy, at a condition preceding monarchy of any kind; is in effect to take the state apart until no single locus of authority remains, but rather as many loci as nobles. Not even the monarchomachs desired such an anarchic situation.

Thus where the monarchomachs argue for a *mixture* or equilibration of the primary forms of aristocracy and monarchy, our fable tells of a *lapse* from pure aristocracy into pure or unconditioned monarchy—discovers a chasm between the two simple forms the monarchomachs would integrate, assigning one to the past exclusively and one to the present exclusively, and, while indulging via the Golden Age echoes a certain nostalgia for the past, finally contraindicating any plans for even a partial comeback of the lapsed form ("in patience bide your hell"). By omitting the middle term, Sidney leaves out the core of the monarchomach program. His divergence from the radicals resides less in his choice between the resulting two simple forms (although I don't see that the community has much choice) than in his suggestion that the two forms exclude each other. Man's present political lot, Sidney's text seems to suggest, is ineluctably Iron. If so, I do not see how Hubert Languet can be held accountable for it.

[19]François Hotman, *Francogallia*, variorum ed. with Latin text by R. A. Giesey, English trans. J. H. M. Salmon (Cambridge: University Press, 1972), p. 142.

[20]Languet, pp. 121–24; also Theodore Beza, *Du droit des magistrats*, ed. Robert M. Kingdon (Geneva: Droz, 1971), pp. 9, 30.

[5]

As an etiological myth describing the origin of kingship, Philisides' fable seems to me to contradict the standard political etiology of the monarchomachs.

These thinkers regularly argued that the state originates when the community freely contracts for a king, stipulating that his mandate will be revoked should he violate certain conditions. Yet royalists too could use contractualist ideas, and did so increasingly through the 1570s to rebut the very thinkers who gave these ideas currency. While agreeing to the hypothesis of an original election, the royalists claimed that this donation of power from the community to a single individual was unilateral, unconditional, and, most important, binding on all future generations. What the community elected, then, was not a single individual but a royal dynasty.[21]

Could this be the sad logic of Sidney's fable too? Did the beasts, when they so vigorously demanded a king, lock themselves into submission for good? Sell not only themselves but also future generations of horses, dogs, and cattle into service to Man? The fable utilizes a biblical episode that seems to me to corroborate such an interpretation.

The beasts' demand for a king (11. 56–77) parallels that of Israel in 1 Samuel 8. The parallel between these two episodes involves not only the demand for a king but also its context, its outcome, and its implications.

In both texts the community's demand for a king is spontaneous, having little more cause than did the Fall itself. In both texts the demand incurs the displeasure of supernatural authority. Israel's demand for a king incurs God's displeasure because it means the community is rejecting his own intrinsic rule in favor of the rule of a

[21] Jean Bodin, *La République* 1.8; Matteo Zampini, *Degli Stati di Francia* (1578) (so G. Weill, *Théories sur le pouvoir royal en France pendant les guerres de religion* [Paris, 1891], p. 191); Claude Fauchet, *Les antiquitez gauloises et françoises* (1579), in *Oeuvres* (1610), p. 195v°; cf. Fauchet's *Origine des dignitez et magistrats de France* (1611), in *Oeuvres*, p. 475v°; François Belleforest, *Grandes Annales de France* (1579), 1:2v°-3r°. This is also the theory of William Barclay, *De regno et regali potestate* (1600), trans. by G. A. Moore as *The Kingdom and the Regal Power* (Chevy Chase, Md.: Country Dollar Press, 1954), pp. 146ff; of Richard Hooker, *The Laws of Ecclesiastical Polity* 1.10.4, 8; 8.2.5, 6, 9, 11; 8.6.8, and cf. Hooker's refutation of the *Vindiciae* specifically, in R. A. Houk (ed.), *Hooker's Ecclesiastical Polity, Book VIII* (New York: Columbia University Press, 1931), pp. 174–75; of Grotius in *De jure belli ac pacis* 1.3.8; and of Pufendorf in *The Whole Duty of Man* 2.6.3, 2.9.2.

single man (cf. 1 Samuel 8.7). For this apostasy God punishes Israel
by subjecting her to the tyrannic rule of the very king she freely
chooses. But first he attempts to dissuade the Israelites by telling
them through Samuel "the maner of the king that shall reign over
them." Jove's warning to the beasts — "O beasts, take heed what you
of me desire./ Rulers will thinke all things made them to please,/ And
soone forget the swincke due to their hire" (11. 72–74) — clearly
echoes God's warning to Israel through his spokesman Samuel that
the king she demands will act ruthlessly:

> This shall be the maner of the king that shall reigne over you: he
> will take your sonnes, and appoint them to his charets, and to be his
> horsemen. . . . He will also take your daughters. . . . And he will
> take your fields, and your vineyards, and your best olive trees . . .
> And he will take your men servants, and your maid servants, and
> the chief of your yong men, and your asses, and put them to his
> work. He will take the tenth of your sheep, and ye shall be his
> servants. And ye shall cry out at that day, because of your king,
> whome ye have chosen you, and the Lord will not heare you at that
> day (1 Samuel 8.11–18, Geneva version).

Both in the Old Testament and in the fable, the community perse-
veres in its demand and receives a king, and the prediction that he
will rule ruthlessly is quickly fulfilled. Both in the Old Testament and
in the fable, the choice of a king marks the irreversible transition
from an aristocratic polity to a monarchic (in scripture, the transition from the priestly aristocracy to Sauline rule and subsequently
the Davidic dynasty). Both the fable and the Old Testament refrain
from outfitting the tyrant with any transcendental trappings, suggesting rather that his dominion is the inevitable consequence of the
people's own desire for a ruler "like the other nations." In neither
text is the ruler amenable to rational correction. For he is not an
"evil" ruler, but any ruler; he is simply the extroversion of the community's desire for submission; he represents at once apostasy from
God and the requisite punishment. Both texts illustrate the central
paradox of the use of freedom to lose freedom.

   What happens in 1 Samuel could never happen in the monarchomach perspective. Given the libertarian myth of inalienable
sovereignty, it is inconceivable that a community would wilfully and
unconditionally remit its rights to a king. Yet this is precisely what

Israel did and what Sidney's beasts do. This is indeed what any community does according to the royalist etiology of the state: at the moment of the original election or *pactum subjectionis* it alienates its power not conditionally to a single individual but once and for all to a line of kings. Thus many royalists who argue for an absolutist theory of contract refer to 1 Samuel for the doctrine that kings have unlimited rights over their subjects.[22] Even the spiritual father of the monarchomachs adduces 1 Samuel as proof that the community has no choice but to obey: John Calvin points out that Samuel's warning ("This will be the maner [in the vulgate, *jus*, right] of the king that shall reign over you") in effect gives free reign to any established monarch; he admits that "kings would not do all this by 'right,' for they were excellently instructed by the law to observe all moderation [cf. Deuteronomy 17]; but it was called a 'right' with respect to the people who were bound to obey, and were not at liberty to resist it. It was just as if Samuel had said, The cupidity of your kings will proceed to all these outrages, which it will not be our province to restrain; nothing will remain for you but to receive their commands and to obey them."[23] Or in other words, "in patience bide your hell."

Sidney's general position in *Arcadia* seems to be that, while the people may have preceded its rulers chronologically, this precedence does not survive the original donation of power. In the case of the Phagonian rebels, Sidney allows Pyrocles to explain in his "pacificatorie oration" that, although the community may have created its first rulers, its primal freedom provides no valid excuse for dissolving its present obligation to Basilius — a dissuasion with which the entire tone of the episode sympathizes (4:124). To turn to external evidence, Sidney rejects the argument from original liberty when the Irish employ it. Defending his father against the charge that his repression of the Irish rebels was unnecessarily severe, Sidney claims (with a brutality the age does not entirely excuse): "untill

---

[22]Cf. Innocent Gentillet (of absolutist tendency though a Politique ally of the Calvinists), *Discours . . . contre Nicolas Machiavel Florentin* (1576), ed. C. Edward Rathé (Geneva: Droz, 1968), p. 87; Adam Blackwood, *Adversus Georgii Buchanani dialogum . . . pro regibus apologia* (1581), in *Opera Omnia* (1644), pp. 140–144; Barclay, pp. 69ff; Grotius 1.3.8.8. This is also Fulke Greville's interpretation of 1 Samuel in his *Treatise of Monarchy*, a work discussed in Appendix B.

[23]Cf. Calvin, *Institutes* 4.20.26, the trans. by John Allen, rev. by Benjamin B. Warfield (Philadelphia: Westminster Press, 1945).

by tyme [the rebels] fynde the sweetenes of dew subjection, it is impossible that any gentle meanes shoolde putt owt the freshe remembrance of their loste lyberty" (3:49). As for Philisides' fable, what Sidney seems to emphasize is the unconditional transfer of the beasts' primal "rights," including, significantly, the gift of speech:

> And aye more awe towards him for to plant,
> To their owne worke this priviledge they graunt,
> That from thenceforth to all eternitie,
> No beast should freely speake, but only he (11. 102–05).

In permanently alienating to the ruler the gift of speech, what do the beasts do but make the noose and place their necks in it? In this regard, Sidney recalls the absolutist construction of 1 Samuel.

One can of course utilize scriptural exempla to just about any purpose. The monarchomachs, who considered such exempla their special province, were aware of the difficulty posed by 1 Samuel and tried to assimilate it into their program. Thus Languet noted impatiently in the *Vindiciae*: "One would hardly believe in what estimation the courtiers of our times hold this text, when of all the rest of Holy Scripture they make but a jest."[24] He attempted to solve the difficulty this exemplum presented by arguing that Samuel's picture of how the king will tyrannize over the people does not, as in Calvin and the royalist "courtiers of our times," amount to a justification of despotic practice, a description of how the choice of kingship will *necessarily* turn out, but just the opposite. Samuel's warning tells what will happen *unless* the king is constrained by definite conditions and can be deposed for violating them.[25]

All the same, it seems that Sidney could hardly have chosen a more troublesome text, one less amenable to the purposes of the monarchomachs. In adducing 1 Samuel, Sidney brings to the fore a scriptural episode Hubert Languet would perhaps have preferred to forget. Yet would Sidney have chosen this text if it had not shared with the monarchomachs the basic postulate (however unredeemable in this case) of the community's creation of its first ruler, and if "old Languet" had not recently had a try at corraling it?

---

[24]Languet, pp. 172–173.
[25]Languet, pp. 172–174; cf. Beza, p. 30.

[6]

I have suggested that the fable at once invites and rejects a libertarian construction. By referring to Languet as its author, the frame stanzas encourage such a construction at the outset. Then four devices within the fable proper continue to invite clarification in the light of the king-fighters, viz., an appropriately blood-soaked tyrant; a nostalgic evocation of "Such maner time" in terms of the myth of the Golden Age; a clear statement of the fact that the ruler is largely the creation of the community; and an allusion to that favorite hunting ground of the Protestant activists, scriptural history.

Yet further study of each of these devices suggests a political perspective quite at odds with the fable's ostensible source. True, the monarch acts tyrannically; but tyranny does not licence communal revolt. True, things seemed better in "Such maner time"; but back then we were innocent not only of tyrants but indeed of any form of kingship at all — not the monarchomach ideal. True, the community itself brought the monarch into existence; but its creation of the monarch does not presently absolve it from obedience. True, scripture tells a similar story; but it is one that provides little encouragement to king-fighters.

It seems difficult to discuss this text without arriving at ambiguities and obliquities. Should we then use ambiguity itself as a solvent for whatever difficulties the text presents us with? Should we say that the beast-fable works as a "dialogue" between two opposed political traditions — one, that of the monarchomachs; and the other, that of the legitimists or absolutists — each of which receives equal weight? Although the fable is ambiguous in the sense that it is recalcitrant, invites different readings, I do not think that it is ambiguous in the sense that all of these readings are equally valid. In fact, I think the balance tips decisively when we adduce a piece of evidence that has been under our noses all along. This resides in the principal change Sidney has effected in his scriptural model, his substitution of a populace of beasts for the Israelite petitioners. Such a substitution introduces Sidney's most original and definitive transvaluation of "old Languet."

CHAPTER FIVE

Man Was Not Man

Philisides' Fable II

... some god's compassion
set a big buck in motion to cross my path —
a stag with noble antlers, pacing down
from pasture in the woods to the riverside,
as long thirst and the power of sun constrained him.
He started from the bush and wheeled: I hit him
square in the spine midway along his back
and the bronze point broke through it. In the dust
he fell and whinnied as life bled away.
                    —*Odyssey* trans. Robert Fitzgerald

This product is guaranteed to contain no substance of animal origin
                                        —a margarine label

[1]

FOR THE MANNER IN WHICH MAN SHOULD RELATE to the beasts,
Sidney has two traditions available to him. Both agree on one
point — that once upon a time Man lived in perfect harmony with,
indeed was almost indistinguishable from, the animal kingdom.
Both agree that this harmony was eventually shattered when Man
turned savagely on his former friends and enslaved them to his own
use and pleasure, an enslavement or subordination that endures to
the present day. The two traditions disagree in their judgment of
the present situation — one censuring Man's use of the animal kingdom and calling for a return to the prelapsarian respect and harmony, and the other representing Man's utilization of the beasts as a
necessary if regrettable precondition of his civility, of his advance

79

from the original state, which this tradition represents as brutish
and primitive rather than idyllic.

The first tradition, which I shall call the primitivist one, argues
that Man has no right to make free with the lives of animals for food,
skins, or any other purpose. For sustenance he has vegetables; these
obviate the need for him to depend on animal meat. A famous
exponent of this view was Pythagoras, the Greek philosopher of the
sixth century B.C., who enjoined vegetarianism on all members of
his school, and the *locus classicus* for this view is the great speech that
Ovid gives to Pythagoras in Book Fifteen of the *Metamorphoses*:

> There was a time, the Golden Age, we call it,
> Happy in fruits and herbs, when no men tainted
> Their lips with blood, and birds went flying rapidly
> Through air, and in the fields the rabbits wandered
> Unfrightened . . .
>   . . . all things
> Were free from treachery and fear and cunning,
> And all was peaceful. But some innovator,
> A good-for-nothing, whoever he was, decided,
> In envy, that what lions ate was better,
> Stuffed meat into his belly like a furnace,
> And paved the way for crime. . . .[1]

The second tradition, which I shall call the progressivist one, dismisses this attitude as viciously sentimental. It claims that if Man
could be said to have once existed at all "in harmony" with the beasts
of the field, he certainly had not then realized his civilized potential:
to do so he had precisely to begin to differentiate himself from
animal or "natural" existence. This involved acquiring and using
tools and developing the skills of civilized behavior — in short, mod-
ifying his natural inheritance by means of Art. As a corollary to such
modification of his "natural," brutish inheritance, Man would necessarily have had to exploit animal resources since the civilized skills
included those of hunting, fishing, farming, using beasts of burden,
and raising feed animals in captivity. Thus Man provided himself
with cooked meat, skins, and other appurtenances of rational (as
opposed to merely natural) life. Indeed it could be said that Man has
realized his civility in direct proportion to his success in subduing

---

[1] Ovid *Metam*. 15.100–110, trans. Rolfe Humphries (Bloomington: Indiana University Press, 1955), p. 368.

the animal kingdom to his purposes. The progressivist view has several classic expressions in Greek drama as well as in Aristotle. Here Man's subjugation of the beasts is viewed triumphantly:

> Gay nations of birds [Man] snares and leads,
> wild beast tribes and the salty brood of the sea,
> with the twisted mesh of his nets, this clever man.
> He controls with craft the beasts of the open air,
> walkers on hills. The horse with his shaggy mane
> he holds and harnesses, yoked about the neck,
> and the strong bull of the mountain.[2]

> I first brought beasts under the yoke, that with bodies
> bowed to the collar they might relieve mortals of their
> greatest toil, and brought horses to the chariot, obedient
> to the reins, to be the glory of wealth and luxury.[3]

> We may infer that . . . animals exist for the sake of man,
> the tame for use and food, the wild, if not all, at least
> the greater part of them, for food, and for the provision
> of clothing and various instruments.[4]

Each of these two views quickly implicates larger questions regarding the course of history (fall from harmony or rise from brutishness?) and Man's purpose. Is Man to live the simplest existence possible or the most differentiated and artful?

* * *

Both of these views — the primitivist as well as the progressivist — leave their imprint on Philisides' beast fable. Upon his creation and installation as ruler, Man adopts, if only momentarily and hypocritically, the primitivist vegetarianism:

> Thus Man was made, thus Man their lord became:
> Who at the first, wanting, or hiding pride,
> He did to beastes' best use his cunning frame;
> *With water drinke, herbes meate, and naked hide,*
> And fellow-like let his dominion slide (11. 106–110, my emphasis).

---

[2]Sophocles *Antigone* 342ff, trans. Elizabeth Wyckoff; D. Grene and R. Lattimore (eds.), *The Complete Greek Tragedies* (Chicago: University of Chicago Press, 1959), Vol. II, pp. 170–171.

[3]Aeschylus *Prometheus Vinctus* 460ff. The trans. is by W. K. C. Guthrie in *The Sophists* (Cambridge: at the Univ. Press, 1971), p. 79.

[4]Aristotle *Politics* 1256B15–23, trans. B. Jowett in Richard McKeon (ed.), *The Basic Works of Aristotle* (New York: Random House, 1941), p. 1137;

Similarly, the campaign of subjugation Man then launches against the animals (ll. 113–48) surely owes something to the lengthy speech of Ovid's Pythagoras describing Man's enthrallment of horses, pigs, cows, sheep, and other animal species (*Met.* 15. 112–142). Finally, Sidney's characterization of the transition from the original "beastlie pollicie" to Man's dominion in terms of the transition from the Golden Age to the Iron Age (several details of which historical scheme also derive from Ovid) also encourages us to think of the primitivist model.

However, although Man's enslavement of the animals to his own purposes recalls the primitivist spirit and is stuffed with allusions to the primitivist model of history (from harmony to disharmony), Sidney's conclusion does not resemble the primitivist one. If the moral of the story for a vegetarian would be that Man should leave off from slaughtering the beasts, this is not precisely the moral for Philisides. As we have seen, Sidney's text nowhere calls for reestablishing the antique harmony or for enfranchising the beasts. On the contrary: Philisides enjoins the beasts to submit to Man's law (1. 153).

Further, the tone of several passages in the fable seems to recall the progressivist view rather than the primitivist view. Consider, for example, the poet's evaluation of the gift donated to Man by the Ape:

> Ape great thing gave, though he did moving stand,
> The instrument of instruments, the hand (ll. 97–98).

Sidney's attitude here is frankly progressivist, insofar as the Ape's contribution to the new, reasoning creature is the most nearly human of all the beasts' gifts, that which permits Man, now provided with tool-grasping hands, to build away from bestiality and cross into culture. Indeed, Sidney is directly quoting Aristotle, one of the premier progressivists, who denominates the hand the "instrument of instruments" (*organon organōn*), i.e., the tool for using tools.[5] Thus all of a sudden Sidney punctures and transvalues the primitivist setting with confident ("great thing") praise of *homo faber*.

Or consider the manner in which Sidney renders Man's subjuga-

---

[5]Cf. Aristotle *De Anima* 432A1–3: "It follows that the soul is analogous to the hand, for as the hand is an instrument of instruments (hē cheir organon estin organōn), so the mind is the form of forms." See also *De partibus animalium* 687A18ff.

tion of the horse and dog, an act that ostensibly testifies to the new
ruler's capricious nature:

> For by and by the horse *faire bitts* did bind:
> The dogge was in a collar taught his kinde (11. 137–38, my em-
> phasis).

Despite the general impression, throughout the enslavement passage, of senseless, gratuitous cruelty, these lines seem to indicate that
Man's corraling of the horse and dog may not have been entirely
arbitrary. That the dog was "*taught* his kinde" may suggest that this
species somehow required Man's rule to realize its nature or its
proper place in the hierarchy; and that the "bitts" that Man forced
on the horse were "faire" ones seems to suggest a positive rather
than a negative evaluation: "*faire*" bits, perhaps, because, although
from one perspective they caused the horse pain, from another they
contributed to the process whereby Man came to control the forces
of what are sometimes called brute nature — "faire" bits because
they contributed to Man's civility. We find ourselves all of a sudden in
the progressivist tradition.

Indeed, for all of its primitivist suggestions, I submit that the
central fact of Sidney's fable is quintessentially progressivist. I am
referring to the fact that in the fable's "before," Man does not exist:
that the fable details his coming-to-be. Since Man develops only as a
direct result of the beasts' alienation of their individual qualities plus
Jove's "fire," since Man is a derived or eventual phenomenon, then
the fable cannot, ironically, be other than progressivist. It is the
essence of the progressivist position that Man comes to be in the
course of history, that he acquires his humanity only by distinguishing himself from the natural, undifferentiated, original condition.
Man is essentially an "after," not a "before" — a result of the progressive, if painful, separation from the zero ground of the animals.
"Before" may have been happy, but it was the happiness of inanity,
artlessness, and innocence; whatever animals "before" boasted, Man
could not have been one of them, for he could only arrive by transcending such innocence. The very first stanza of Sidney's fable ends
by reminding us of Man's *absence* from the original condition:

> Such maner time there was (what time I n'ot)
> When all this Earth, this damme or mould of ours,

Was onely won'd with such as beastes begot:
Unknowne as then were they that buylden towers:
The cattell wild, or tame, in nature's bowers
   Might freely rome, or rest, as seemed them:
Man was not man their dwellings in to hem (11. 43–49, my emphasis).

Man, then must supervene on the original condition. By brilliantly combining the Prometheus myth (an essentially progressivist item) with Israel's demand for a king, Sidney has him do so as a direct result of the beasts' petition to Jove (11. 57–105). Thus our fable functions as an etiological myth detailing the origin of Man.

It should be noted that the previous paragraph is not evaluative or critical but simply descriptive. That Sidney's version of history here is finally, for all the suggestions of a lapse from Gold to Iron, the progressivist one, stems directly from the simple fact that Man is absent from the Gold. One may object that the fable couldn't possibly be endorsing the movement from Gold to Iron because this movement involves submitting the animals to a great deal of pain and cruelty. To this objection the text answers that such pain and cruelty, insofar as it is secondary to Man's progressive definition of himself, is acceptable and necessary. Sidney obviously does not make light of the suffering of the animals or suggest that all of it can be assumed into Man's purpose and end. He allows that it is compounded of the purposeful (which may be excused) and the gratuitous (which may not). This is the point, I think, of his distinguishing two moments in Man's use of the animals for food:

> *For hungrie throte* their flesh with teeth he brused:
> At length *for glutton taste* he did them kill: (11. 145–46, my emphasis).

Where "glutton taste" provides an unacceptable motive for Man's killing animals, "hungrie throte" may not. Spilling beasts' "sillie lives" "for sport" (1. 147) sounds capricious; but then, as we have seen, "faire bitts" bind the horse.

Although the beasts' subservience involves pain — and we must give Sidney credit for not overlooking this point — there is no question whatsoever of exempting them from this subservience once Man has secured it. His enslavement of the beasts is not "natural," but only in the sense that it is not aboriginal; it develops in the course of time. Once realized, however, this enslavement is natural in the sense that it is an integral part of Man's definition: reverse it, return to the beasts their primal qualities, and you undo him. Thus the ultimate position of the fable is compatible with the hoariest of commonplaces regarding Man's rightful dominion, as exclusive possessor of that transcendent "heav'nly fire" lent him by his maker, "beyond and over all the works" of nature including the beasts of the field.[6] When the beasts gave over their rights, then, they did so permanently: they bound not only themselves but also all of their descendents into service to Man and his seed, with a result that can be observed in kitchens and tanneries in Sidney's time. Presently, as the poet puts it elsewhere in *Arcadia*,

> the beast
> . . . bears the bit a weaker force doth guide,
> Yet patient must abide

— the "weaker force" being, of course, Man.[7] His dominion is no longer open to challenge. As we have seen in previous chapters, the argument from "lost liberty" does not impress Sidney in Helots, Phagonian commoners, or Irishmen, and now we see that it does not impress him in beasts either.

The theme of Man's eventual rightful dominion over the beasts pervades Renaissance literature and iconography. It may be helpful to mention a single example. My frontispiece, Piero di Cosimo's "Forest Fire," forms the third and last in a series of panels illustrating this evolutionistic theme: to realize himself, Man must transcend and subdue his bestial aspect. The primal state, depicted in the first panel (not shown), features a wierd amalgam of man-beasts mating, fighting, and killing indiscriminately. In the second panel (not shown), a certain advance is evident: Man has differentiated himself from the beasts sufficiently to halt the killing and to take the first steps in mastering physical nature. But he can as yet only hunt

---

[6]Philip Sidney, *Apology for Poetry* (London: Nelson, 1965), p. 101; cf. Gen. 1:26; Hebr. 2:17; Ps. 8.

[7]Jean Robertson (ed.), *The Countess of Pembroke's Arcadia* (*The Old Arcadia*) (Oxford: Clarendon Press, 1973), p. 63; William A. Ringler, Jr. (ed.), *The Poems of Sir Philip Sidney* (Oxford: Clarendon Press, 1962), p. 20; or A. Feuillerat (ed.), *Prose Works of Sir Philip Sidney* (Cambridge: University Press, 1962), 4:59. The notion of Man's being physically weaker than the beasts is a Renaissance conventionalism. We find it, for example, in Fulke Greville's *Treatise of Monarchy*, a work discussed in Appendix B.

animals, not domesticate them; lacking tools, he cannot manufac-
ture a true shelter; lacking woven material, he goes clad in skins; a
forest fire ravaging the woods illustrates his unfamiliarity with fire,
control of which is a key condition of technology. In our panel, the
third and last, Man prepares to advance definitively into civilization.
While the forest fire recurs, scattering the strange creatures that
result from the promiscuous mating of man-beasts, it no longer
frightens Man himself, who advances confidently in the middle
plane. Wearing a coarse leather coat unstead of uncured skins, he
prepares to catch some of the cows and oxen that have fled from the
burning woods — to domesticate these creatures rather than merely
to hunt them. For on his shoulder he providently carries their future
yoke, the thematic equivalent of Sidney's "faire bitts."[8]

[2]

What does all this have to do with Hubert Languet and the king-
fighters? Everything. Where the last chapter dealt with the fable as
an etiological myth concerning the origin of the state, this one has
begun by dealing with it as an etiological myth concerning the origin
of Man. Lack of attention to the latter aspect has been responsible
for confusing the political aspect of Sidney's fable. When we discussed the political aspect of the fable, we were hampered by the
absence of any editorial or normative context: we could do little
more than note some discrepancies between Languet's position and
the fable's. But it was difficult to do much more than that: to any of
my suggestions that the text inclines to a position opposite from
Languet's, one could always answer, Yes, but even on your own
reckoning the fable cues as often toward Languet as away from him;
and who is to help us to decide which interpretation to favor? The
answer is Sidney: for the aspect of the fable pertaining to the etiology of Man provides an editorial or normative apparatus which
allows us to resolve the aspect pertaining to the state.

Thus: the assumption of critics heretofore has generally been that
Sidney is representing the "beastly pollicie" as an ideal from which
Man's rule constitutes a lapse and proposing as a means of mitigat-

[8]For the evolutionistic, or what I have been calling "progressivist," view of Piero's
cycle, see Erwin Panofsky, *Studies in Iconology* (New York: Harper & Row, 1962), pp.
33–67.

ing that lapse the resurrection of those aristocratic "great beasts" who once exercised authority — a proposition that was Languet's. But in view of what we have learned by attending to the fable as a creation myth concerning Man, this cannot be the right way of going about it. For now we know that the fable depicts the progressive coming-to-be of Man, not a lapse from harmony; now we see that the fable is arguing for anything but a return to the pristine condition; now we see that the fable defines Man in terms of where it ends (he has, thanks to the animals, beasts of burden, transportation, clothing, food, pets, and games) rather than in terms of where it began (he didn't exist). Given that the fable defines the norm in terms of where it ends (the norm is Man) rather than in terms of where it began (when there weren't any norms), then — moving to the political level — the political norm must be secure at the conclusion of the fable rather than at the beginning.

Does this mean that the political norm or ideal for Sidney is tyranny? No, it does not — not exactly. First, it means that, in terms of the opposition between the "before" of aristocracy and the "after" of unlimited monarchy, the "after" is vastly preferable. The "before" indeed doesn't qualify as anything that would be of even the slightest use to a monarchy, because it is *pure* aristocracy or noble-centered rule, with as many loci of power as nobles, and therefore a condition prior to the state as Sidney would define it, one reminiscent of the situation that obtains when centralized rule lapses and power returns into the hands of the feudal nobility, as in England during the Wars of the Roses or in France during the Civil Wars.

Second, the violence that the consolidation of Man's rule involves — a violence that Sidney does anything but blink away — has nonetheless a positive aspect. This is as true on the political level of Sidney's fable as it is on what may be called its cultural. For this violence obtains at the state's *moment of origin.* To establish the state, the centrifugal, anomic tendencies of the great feudal lords must be checked, and they can only be checked by a series of swift, decisive, and perhaps violent acts — in no other way can the state be integrated, given definition, identity, and a single locus. This is not at all to say that the ordinary function of the monarch is to act brutally. Indeed, once he has secured order, the necessity for violence diminishes. But the fable does not tell us of the peace that the initial violence secures — though Man must terrorize the first generation of beasts, his seed need not terrorize theirs, just as breaking a horse is infinitely more traumatic than riding its offspring—simply because that is not its subject. Its subject is the state's inaugural violence.

This is the subject as well of another episode in Sidney's *Arcadia* (the *New Aracadia* this time), one that it is helpful to consider presently because the poet makes the point fairly explicitly rather than under the cover of a fable. I am referring to King Euarchus' violent subjugation of the Macedonian nobles, an action that seems to me to receive Sidney's entire approval on the ground that it is crucial to the subsequent establishment of peace in Euarchus' monarchy. (Indeed, not only does the name "Euarchus" mean "good ruler," but also the chapter heading commends his "kingly excellencies," and he plays the principal heroic role at the denouement of the *Old Arcadia*, one that he was surely destined to repeat at the denouement of the *New*.) This passage also serves to remind us that the condition of "before," the anarchic rule of the feudal nobility, can happen any time, is not confined to "Such maner time," *illud tempus*—it happens each time central authority relaxes.

In the case of Macedonia, an interregnum had seen sovereignty revert to the rule of the "great Lords" and thus to the "worst kind of *Oligarchie*," with unfortunate results for the entire kingdom: "Hence grew a very dissolution of all estates, while the great men (by the nature of ambition never satisfied) grew factious among themselves. . . . Men of vertue suppressed; marchandise abused . . . townes decayed . . . offices . . . solde; publique defences neglected; and in summe . . . all awrie" (1:186). Thus when Euarchus assumed rulership, he was forced to establish order "by some even extreme severitie." However, "so soone as some fewe (but in deede notable) examples, had thundred a duetie into the subjects hartes," Euarchus was able to mitigate the violence of inauguration: "then shined foorth indeede all love among them, when an awfull feare, ingendred by justice, did make that love most lovely. . . . So that within small time, he wanne a singular love in his people, and engrafted singular confidence" (1:186–87). To secure this love and confidence he had at the moment of the institution of his rule to play the part of violence—the same sorry but necessary part that Man plays in our fable.[9]

---

[9]Note that the Euarchus passage contains a reminiscence of the metaphor of the ruler as caretaker of beasts which operates in the fable: "[Euarchus] even in reason disdayning, that they that have charge of beastes, should love their charge, and care for them; and that he that was to governe the most excellent creature, should not love so noble a charge" (1:187).

To bring his kingdom into focus, Man, like Euarchus, must crush
the great nobles. So far from calling for the rehabilitation of these
"nobler beastes," Sidney is making their vigilant repression a precondition of law and order. This reading has the virtue of bringing
Sidney's fable into harmony with every other page of *Arcadia*, and of
obviating the need that critics have felt to apologize for what they
saw as the fable's unusual praise of aristocracy.[10] In fact, Sidney
regularly and consistently regards the feudal nobility with the utmost suspicion. As we have seen in the case of the Amphialus
episode, he perceives no greater threat to the welfare of the state
than the nobles' arrogation of power to themselves, and his ironic
attitude to the aristocratic cult of martial glory provides a unifying
motive for much of Arcadian intrigue. To this generally antiaristo-
cratic, pro-monarchic attitude, the fable is no exception. Indeed it
provides an Aesopic defense of Politique, centralized monarchy,
emphasizing the community's unequivocal alienation of sovereignty
to a moderately though not arbitrarily absolute executive, an alienation that is principally at the expense of those great feudal nobles to
whom the king-fighters, including "old Languet," looked for salva-
tion.

This is not to say that Sidney does not tempt us in the primitivist
(or, in political terms, the aristocratic) direction. He does so to allow
us to recapitulate Languet's conception of politics. As I have suggested all along, Sidney never dismisses the monarchomachs as, say,
Bodin did. Rather he extends his reader an invitation to consider
the consequences of the monarchomach position. Just as Amphialus
must have his moment of plausibility, so must Languet. In the fable
Sidney invests Languet's position, then, with all the attractiveness
and plausibility of that which is Natural, primal, and aboriginal.
Only when we subsume the political question under the more inclusive one of Art and Nature — a question that unifies everything Sidney writes including *Astrophil and Stella* and the *Apology for Poetry* —
can we appreciate that Sidney's defense of Man as derived, eventual,
or artificial involves a concomitant rejection of Languet's position.

Rejection, indeed of the "beastly pollicie." To engage the fable's
cultural progressivism is to arrive at the conclusion that aristocracy is
a beastly political order in the pejorative sense of the word whereas
monarchy is a humane one. In the next section of my essay, I shall

[10]Norman Levine, "Aspects of Moral and Political Thought in Sidney's *Arcadia*"
(Ph.D. dissertation, Columbia University, 1972), p. 132.

try to show that Sidney' text continually reminds us of the
dichotomy between beast and Man and asks for clarification in terms
of that dichotomy, with that which partakes of the bestial to be
judged as defective and that which partakes of Man as normative.
The distinction between beast and Man, then, is not simply what the
fable concerns on a narrative level (the narrative explaining how this
distinction arose); it is also a category or lens in terms of which the
fable invites criticism and interpretation.

[3]

Consider the beasts' "speech." The poet claims that, prior to the
beasts' fall into the service of Man and monarchy, "their language
was a perfect speech" (1. 65). But this statement comes as a par-
enthesis in the description of the beasts' manner of petitioning Jove,
a description that undercuts the parenthetical claim by suggesting
that the beasts, so far from owning a perfected speech, can only
produce animal noises:

> The multitude to Jove a suite empartes,
>   With neighing, blaying, braying, and barking,
>   Roring, and howling for to have a King.
>
> A King, in language theirs they said they would:
> (For then their language was a perfect speech)
> The birdes likewise with chirpes, and puing could,
> Cackling, and chattring, that of Jove beseech (11. 61–67).

Do "neighing, blaying, braying, and barking,/Roring, and howling,"
"chirp[ing], and puing," "Cackling, and chattering" comprise "perfect speech"? Rather these lines remind us of the discontinuity between beastly noises on the one hand and human speech and reason,
ratio et oratio, on the other — a discontinuity repeatedly emphasized
in the progressivist tradition but useless to the primitivists, the origin
of which the fable explains by noting Jove's donation of reason (his
"heav'nly fire") to Man alone.
    The disjunct between the beastly and the human organizes even
the metrical structure in these lines, as the normative pattern of
alternate weak- and strong-stressed syllables, significantly most
nearly fulfilled in the parenthetical 1. 65 —

Fŏr thēn |thĕir lān | guăge wās |ă pēr | fĕct spēech

is violently disrupted by the speech-stress or ictus precisely at those points where the beasts make noises:

Rŏrīng, ănd hōwlĭng |fōr tŏ hăve ă Kīng (1. 63).

Căcklīng, ănd chāttrĭng, |thāt ŏf Jōve bĕsēech (1. 67).

With neíghing, |bláying, |bráying, |and bárking (1. 62).

The beasts tend to force trochees against the iambic norm (róring, cáckling, bárking, etc.); disruption of the normal caesural structure — these lines tend to section after the fifth rather than the fourth syllable — also gives an awkward trochaic lilt. With 1. 62, the effect is so pronounced as completely to obfuscate the metrical norm, resulting in something like four-beat accentual verse. Such violent disruption of the metrical norm is obviously intentional, as it is a local effect, occurring only in these lines — indeed nowhere else in Sidney's verse. It works to reinforce the suggestion that the beasts, so far from fulfilling order or reason, represent its antithesis.

Sidney draws attention to the disjunct between what is animal and what is human in other ways. For example, the fable's dramatic context, or the "frame" stanzas, contain a witty reminder of this disjunct. Recall that Philisides' occupation is that of shepherd, and that his primary audience is a wooly one ("As I my little flocke . . . /Did piping leade . . . "). Thus the fable's context assumes precisely that relationship between Man and beast — Man guides and beasts follow — the origin of which the fable accounts for. I said that you could see the results of the original *pactum subjectionis* in kitchens and tanneries: you may also see it in pastures (and in the literary genre of pastoral). There, Man's original act of aggression ("Worst fell to . . . meanest heard,/ Who now his owne, full like his owne he used./ Yet first but wooll . . . he teard" [11. 141–43]) having been normalized, the sheep presently yield their coats without complaint.

Yet if we are to judge by the *first* of the frame stanzas, Philisides' sheep seem unusual in one respect:

As I my little flocke on Ister banke
(A little flocke, *but well my pipe they couthe*)
Did piping leade . . . (11. 1–3, emphasis mine).

These sheep seem to possess the rational faculty, they "couthe" — understood — Philisides' pipe well. This contraindicates the general suggestion of a discontinuity between beasts and Man. Yet by the *last* of the frame stanzas, that following the fable, Sidney is at pains to refute this suggestion directly:

> Thus did I singe, and pipe eight sullen houres
> To sheepe, *whom love, not knowledge, made to heare,*
> Now fancie's fits, now fortune's baleful stowers: (11. 155–57, my emphasis).

The sheep, then, "heare" only in the sense that they gather submissively around their guardian; their rational apprehension the poet now explicitly rules out; reason and knowledge are Man's business, a fact of which the fable reminds us continually and of which, not coincidentally, Sidney reminds a friend in May 1580, or about the time he is composing "Ister banke": "The delighte of knowledge," he writes to Ned Denny," is one of the notablest effects of that, which makes us differ from beasts."[11] That Philisides' sheep listen to the song with "love, not knowledge" is another of many witty reminders in the text of the discontinuity between beasts and Man. In this regard, to read the fable is to learn to progress from the statement in the opening stanza that the sheep "couthe" Philisides' pipe to the statement in the closing stanza that they heard with "love, not knowledge"; is to detach oneself from Philisides' "lambkins deare" and to range oneself with the men in his audience — for Philisides is also repeating the fable to the crew of Arcadian shepherds — who have at least the presence of mind to ask "what hee shoulde meane by yt" (4:242). Readers and auditors differ from sheep by virtue of possessing reason. And if there is no continuity between beasts on the one hand and reader-auditors on the other, then there is no relationship between the "beastly" policy and ours; and Sidney, rather than calling for a re-creation of that policy in the present, rejects it.

[4]

Yet Philisides does not. Thus we must distinguish Philisides, the speaker of the poem, from Philip Sidney, its author. This is a distinc-

---

[11]This letter was first printed in James Osborn, *Young Philip Sidney* (New Haven: Yale University Press, 1972), p. 537.

tion for which there is ample precedent in Sidney's works. As I noted earlier, modern criticism regularly distinguishes between Astrophil, the speaker of the great sonnet sequence *Astrophil and Stella*, and its author. Through the "aesthetic distance" that obtains between the maundering Astrophil and the skeptical poet, one could comfortably drive a small critical library.[12]

The same holds true for "the lad Philisides," a sentimental shepherd, as opposed to his creator, who was anything but sentimental. Philisides may be defined as the part of Sidney that heard Languet and believed. That Sidney heard Languet expound his ideas, I have no doubt, and this much of the frame stanzas is painstakingly accurate — a direct reflection of the poet's experience:

> With old true tales [Languet] woont mine eares to fill,
> How sheepheards did of yore, how now they thrive,
> Spoiling their flocke, or while twixt them they strive.

Too much critical energy has been expended on discovering a precise historical meeting between Sidney and Languet which would underlie these lines as well as Philisides' singing of the fable "on Ister banke" (i.e., in Vienna). First, the fiction refers to two separate occasions, not one (there is the time when Languet teaches Philisides the fable, referred to in ll. 22–42, and then there is the time when Philisides in turn sings the fable to his flock, referred to in the remaining lines), and, while the second of these fictional occasions doesn't seem to me to call for any historical or extrafictional reference at all, the first — Languet's teaching the young Sidney — may have more than a single such reference. Writing in 1580, Sidney was remembering, I think, a number of occasions on which Languet expounded his ideas regarding the nature of the state: he was remembering the winter of 1574–75 when, at Michael Lingelsheim's house in Vienna, he heard Estienne and Languet hold the discussion referred to in the Preface of the *Vindiciae contra tyrannos*; or the spring of 1577, when Languet, frustrated from publishing the completed *Vindiciae* by Anjou's desertion of the Huguenots, spent several refreshing weeks with Sidney ("I felt incredible satisfaction from our intercourse during so many days"[13]), during the course of

---

[12]A recent essay by Alan Sinfield, "Sidney and Astrophil," *Studies in English Literature* 20 (1980), 25–42, provides a summary of scholarly opinion on the relationship between Sidney and his *persona* and makes a strong case for a disjunctive relation.

[13]Languet to Sidney, June 14, 1577; in *The Correspondence of Philip Sidney and Hubert Languet*, trans. S.A. Pears (London, 1845).

which time one finds it hard to believe that he did not share some of
his frustrations and political aspirations, not to mention his manuscript, with the poet; or February of 1579, the last time Sidney would
see Languet alive, at the conclusion of which they "made many
mutual tears ominous propheciers of their never meeting again."[14]
More important than providing a specific historical occasion for
Languet's teaching the young Sidney "the origin and growth of
states" (as Daniel Rogers in 1579 reported he did)[15] is noting how
well Philisides' description of Languet's "old true tales" corresponds
to the *Vindiciae contra tyrannos* and to monarchomach thought in
general. "How sheepheards did *of yore*, how *now* they thrive,/ Spoiling their flocke . . ." — here in a nutshell is one of the central monarchomach strategies, which consists in censuring present-day rulers
in the light of the putative justice that obtained in days "of yore."
Sidney had been exposed to this strategy in innumerable ways; he
had heard it countless times from Languet and various other allies
on the continent; and months prior to writing the fable he saw it
published to the world as the *Vindiciae*. Surely it was the publication
of this work that encouraged Sidney to provide an analysis of its
central idea in *Arcadia*.

He had by this time little sympathy with its ideas, if indeed he had
ever had any, and yet a great deal of sympathy for its author, whom
he had once written that he considered as a father. Out of this
dialectical tug between personal involvement and judgment came
Philisides and the fable. The fable turns on the same distinction
between the days "of yore" and the present adverted to in the frame
stanzas, and its speaker is one of Sidney's central devices for suscitat-
ing a primitivist, nostalgic response, since Philisides, like Languet,
prefers the unspoiled to the derivative or eventual condition. But
Philisides is a *naif*, who does not know that the fable he recites to his

---

[14]Fulke Greville, *Life of Sir Philip Sidney* (Oxford: Clarendon Press, 1907), p. 10.

[15]Cf. J. A. van Dorsten, *Poets, Patrons, and Professors* (London: Oxford University
Press, 1962), p. 65. For various attempts to provide a specific date for Languet's
teaching Philisides, cf. Ringler, pp. 412–414, and Robertson, p. 463. These editors
have been led astray, I think, by the assumption that this must have occurred in
Vienna (on "Ister banke") and in the month of August (cf. 1. 14), neither of which is
necessarily true. For while Vienna, as Languet's primary diplomatic post and the site
of much of his instruction of Sidney, offers a convenient locus for the fable, their
discussions elsewhere (e.g., Germany and England) may also be apposite to its theme
and need not be excluded. On a related issue, see Appendix B in regard to the
identity of Coredens (1. 40). As for the reference to the month of August, see note 16
below.

sheep, so far from faithfully reproducing the position of his mentor, "old Languet," transvalues it. But this is not for Philisides to know, or for any of those "whom love, not knowledge, made to heare." It is for the reader to know. In the parlance of modern criticism, there is aesthetic distance between the speaker of the poem and its author.

It seems to me that the text wittily alludes to Philisides' *naiveté*, indeed his utter incomprehension, in a number of specific ways. What Philisides ignores is the manner in which the dichotomy of beast versus Man serves not only as a descriptive but also as an evaluative category, and indeed judges him and his primitivism. Consider, for example, his praise of the pristine condition. Even this contains an ironic qualifier, although he himself is unaware of it. Philisides looks at the "beastly pollicie" and pronounces it good:

> This thinke I well, the beasts with courage clad
> Like Senators a harmeles empire had (11. 55–56).

His "This thinke I well" is praise to the beasts for realizing an equitable, "harmeles" form of government. (Whether "well" is a predicate adjective — "I think this good" — or an intensive adverb — "I am good at thinking this" — the expression is undeniably a value judgment on the part of Philisides.) However, emphasis falls at the same time on the fact that Philisides is *thinking*, that is, exercising the faculty of reason, his Jove-given (11. 75–76) gift appointing him Man *rather than* beast. Thus he *differentiates* himself from the beasts even while praising them, or testifies to the very distinction between beast and Man to which, as we have seen, the fable recurs repeatedly and which indeed allows us to pronounce his own judgment to be defective in this case — since he is imputing something ("pollicie") to the beasts that on the fable's own terms they cannot display.

Further, the metrical structure of the line

> This thinke I well,// the beasts with courage clad

reinforces the same disjunct between the animal and the rational orders: a pronounced caesura sections four syllables of Man and thought from six of beasts and "courage" (i.e., sheer physical strength). (Again, the effect is significant only because it is local: hardly any other line in the poem displays such an emphatic caesura precisely where the sixteenth century norm calls for one.) Semantically, syntactically, and metrically, the line segregates

Philisides as a thinking observer or subject (four syllables' worth) over against the beasts as irrational objects (six syllables' worth); this dis-continuity between Man and beasts contradicts Philisides' whole attempt to map from "beastly" policy into human.

One symptom of his *naiveté*, then, consists in his projecting human qualities onto animals, perceiving in the rule of the merely "courageous," or physically powerful, beasts over the "weaker sort" (1. 121) the configuration of a human Senate (1. 56). (The irony cuts both against Philisides for exercising a variant of the "pathetic fallacy" as well as against those modern readers who recapitulate his error by instantly perceiving a certain human "policy" in the bestial configuration.) Indeed, Philisides is so foolish that he thinks glowworms shine in the dark because they are being "curteous" to shepherds (11. 6-7).

Through a number of allusions Sidney exposes Philisides' utter lack of knowledge as well as of self-knowledge. These involve the frame stanzas rather than the fable itself. Students of the literary genre of pastoral may notice one striking peculiarity in Philisides' conduct. Unlike most normal literary shepherds who sing songs to their flock, Philisides sings his fable *at night*:

> As I my little flocke on *Ister* banke
> . . . .
> Did piping leade, the Sunne already sanke
> Beyond our worlde, and ere I gatt my boothe
> Each thing with mantle black the night doth soothe;
>   Saving the glowe worme, which would curteous be
>   Of that small light oft watching shepheards see.
>
> The welkin had fully niggardly enclosed
> In cofer of dimme clowdes his silver groates,
> Icleped starres; each thing to rest disposed:
> The caves were full, the mountaines voide of goates:
> The birds' eyes closde, closed their chirping notes.
>   As for the Nightingale, woodmusique's King,
>   It *August* was, he daynde not then to sing.
>
> Amid my sheepe, though I sawe nought to feare,
> Yet (for I nothing sawe) I feared sore;
> Then founde I which thing is a charge to beare
> For for my sheepe I dreaded mickle more
> Then ever for my selfe since I was bore:
>   I sate me downe: for see to goe ne could,
>   And sang unto my sheepe lest stray they should (11. 1, 3-21).

Finally, having recited his fable through "eight sullen houres" of pitch-black darkness (to an audience, as we've seen, ill-equipped to appreciate it since possessed of "love not knowledge"), Philisides "homeward [calls his] lambkins deare" at the first sign of sunrise:

> For to my dimmed eyes beganne t'appeare
> The night growne old, her blacke head waxen gray,
> Sure shepheard's sign, that morne would soone fetch day (11. 158–61).

For literary shepherds, not to speak of real ones, this is perverse behavior. The pastoral tradition to Sidney's knowledge of which every page of *Arcadia* bears witness regularly features a shepherd who sings to his sheep during the day-time (generally when the sun is highest in the sky, thus causing the shepherd to seek shade under a tree and take out his "pipe" [cf. Virgil's *Eclogues*, the seminal work in the genre, for several examples]). The end of the day, then, is the fitting moment for the shepherd to round up his charge and head home (cf. Virgil, *Eclogues* 10. 118). Philisides' night-time piping and taking his sheep home at sunrise turns the tradition upside down. Given Sidney's exquisite modulation of the genre in so many other instances, such a gross change cannot be without meaning. Philisides' substitution of night for day testifies (a) to his incompetence as a shepherd and therefore as a leader, and (b) to his own state of mind, where fear (11. 15–16), dread (1. 18), and confusion reign. We take him as our guide through the fable at our own risk.

Further testifying, I think, to Philisides' confusion, and funny besides, is the manner in which he knots himself up in fancy Spenserianisms here. Thus his conceited description of an overcast night as the "welkin's" enclosing "In cofer of dimme clowdes his silver groates" works well enough until he suddenly loses his balance and falls into plain nonmetaphorical English — "his silver groates,/ Icleped *starres*" (11. 8–10). Such a quick shift of linguistic levels leaves us with an uneasy sense of the gap between the highfalutin archaisms — stylistic cognate of Philisides' sentimental nostalgia for "such maner time" — and the plainer realities. "Silver groates" is Philisides; "starres" is Sidney.

A famous clue for Sherlock Holmes involves a dog that doesn't bark. A clue for us, and final testimony to Philisides' obtuseness, involves the Nightingale that doesn't sing — or so Philisides avers:

As for the Nightingale, woodmusique's King,
It *August* was, he daynde not then to sing (11. 13–14).

Collectors of literary, not to speak of real, Nightingales should instantly cry foul. Sidney, I think, specifies an August night by way of locating Philisides' recital to his sheep in that very season of the year — high summer — when the Nightingale is known to sing most exuberantly. (Keats' "Thou . . . singest of summer in full-throated ease" has both literary precedent and naturalistic justification.) Assume, then, that the bird sings; the question is why Philisides proves deaf to it. His deafness signals his utter divorce not only from his bestial charge but from the entire natural world; so intent has he been on detecting anthropomorphic predilection in bestial behavior (the bird "dayn[s] not," no less) that he's missed the simplest seasonal imperative; he proves no better at telling summer from winter (when the bird truly is quiet) than day from night. To look further in this direction is to encounter the traditional identification between the Nightingale's lyric and the poet's (guess whence Man derives the gift of "voice, entising songes to saye," 1. 82?), and then to realize that Philisides' deafness to the bird defines his ignorance of the very "songe" he sings — he doesn't *comprehend* the fable to which he gives voice, any more than the silly sheep do. Thus the Nightingale's *absence* to Philisides demarcates the distance between speaker, who doesn't know the first thing about nature or pastoral, and poet, who has read and lived the books, knows the conventions, puts the bird in the wood, and causes it — on every other English summer night and for all other ears but Philisides' — to sing.[16]

* * *

By representing the Philisides of the frame stanzas as a *naif*, experiencing and reciting matters the true significance of which inevitably escapes him, Sidney prepares us for the duplicitous nature

---

[16]Ringler and Robertson assume that "August" (1. 14) indicates the month in which Languet instructs Philisides. However, "August" clearly indicates the time when Philisides "instructs" his sheep; this event, referred to in 11. 1–21 and 155–61, the poet carefully distinguishes from an earlier one, Languet's originally imparting the fable to Philisides, referred to in 11. 22–42 (the earlier event, for example, happens under an oak tree during the day [cf. 1. 41] whereas the later one happens at night). While Languet's teaching Philisides admits of historical reference, I don't feel that this is true of Philisides' serenading his sheep, and prefer to account for "August" in terms of the internal dynamics of the fable. This calls for the speaker to be *temporally* dislocated from nature.

of the fable proper. This means one thing to "old Languet," Philisides himself, as well as any others "whom love, not knowledge made to hear," and quite another to the educated auditor — one well versed in literary convention (pastoral, Spenserian high style, Nightingales) and political reality. To have Philisides and Languet inadvertently pronounce against themselves conduces, I think, to a critique of the monarchomach position that is more intimately effective than any extrinsic rebuttal would be, and that has the virtue — since Philisides stands in relation to Philip Sidney as does Astrophil — of indicating the poet's proximity to the position he refutes.*

* * *

Where Philisides hears Languet and believes, Sidney disbelieves, at least by the time he comes to write *Old Arcadia*. Much as he loves Languet, Sidney considers his political ideas tendentious, abstract, and sentimental at best, and at worst conducive to anarchy. What makes them dangerous is their attempt to rationalize politics, to deny what Christian anthropology calls the Fall:

> [Languet] said, the Musique best thilke powers pleasd
> Was jumpe concorde between our wit and will (ll. 29–30).

Such absolute "concord" between wit and will, the Fall has destroyed. "Our erected wit," Sidney writes in his *Apology for Poetry*,

---

*Finally, a device of a different order than this qualifies the fable's ostensible sympathies. This involves its reception by the audience of Arcadian shepherds, a reception that Sidney pointedly represents as problematic:

> According to the Nature of dyvers Eares, dyvers Judgmentes streight followed, some praysing [Philisides'] voyce, others the wordes, Fitt, to frame a Pastorall style, others the straungenes of the Tale, and scanning what hee shoulde meane by yt: But ould *Geron* who had borne hym a grudge, ever synce in one of theyre *Eglogues* hee had taken hym upp over bitterly, tooke holde of this occasyon to make his Revenge. And sayde hee never sawe thing worse proportioned, then to bring in a Tale of hee knewe not what Beastes at suche a Banquett when rather some Songe of Love or matter for Joyfull melody was to bee broughte forthe: But (sayde hee) this ys the Right Conceipt of a younge Man, who thincke then they speake wyselyest when they can not understand them selves: (4:242).

It is significant, I think, that the one shepherd who takes it upon himself to quarrel with Philisides and insists on his incomprehension of the fable is Geron — that sententious elder who has been viewed as deriving in part from Languet (Ephim Fogel, "The Personal References in the Fiction and Poetry of Sir Philip Sidney" [Ph.D. dissertation, Ohio State University, 1958], pp. 235–40, compares with Geron's defense of "maketh us know what perfection is, and yet our infected will keepeth us from reaching unto it." Man's postlapsarian pride is both symptomized and mitigated by the need for firm extrinsic rule, such rule as Israel chose when she demanded a king.

Symptomized *and* mitigated at once: selective use of "awfull feare" serves as a precondition for Man's civility. Thus his differentiation from the level of the beasts involves a fall and an advance simultaneously. The fable eventuates in a creature who is composite or ambiguous rather than simple, one compounded of celestial *and* bestial; similarly, using the figure of oxymoron, Sidney elsewhere describes Man as a "talking beast" (1:227). From this ambiguous twinning of advance *and* decline, right rule *and* coercion, fear *and* love, rational speech *and* bestiality, Languet attempts to escape into the putative purity and simplicity of times "of yore," an attempt that manifests itself in his fastidiousness ("cleane hands" [1. 25]), a well attested personal trait,[17] no less than in the *Vindiciae*. But such desire for purity generates its opposite: "Qui veut faire l'ange, fait la bête."[18]

---

marriage in a poem immediately following the fable Languet's letter to Sidney of January 8, 1578). Thus, just as Sidney distinguishes Philisides' untutored perception of the fable from our own as educated readers, so he develops an estrangement within "old Languet," making him at once the nominal author of the fable and its most obtuse auditor. That the Languet figure *in the Arcadian audience* so belligerently misses the point of what is nominally his own fable suggests that it isn't his any longer, having been captured and transvalued unbeknownst to him — thanks to the mechanism of aesthetic distance indeed *personae* indeed "speake wyselyest when they can not understand them selves." Another way of putting this is to say that Geron is the "old Languet" figure with his previously implicit alienation from the fable revealed, made patent. I shall not, however, pursue this line of thought any further, first, because it is in the nature of one-to-one correspondences between Arcadian shepherds and historical characters to be imperfect (efforts to sketch such correspondences have tended to be uneven, and I don't find any of them convincing apart from those involving Geron and Philisides) and, second, because the postulated relation between Geron and Languet remains little more than a private gesture on Sidney's part, in decided contrast to the mechanism of "Ister banke" proper, which depends for its ironic point on themes that are (or once were) entirely and vigorously commonplace and public. While Geron is optional, the abiding theme of Man and beast, Nature and Art, is not.

[17]Languet was praised by Melanchthon for his "austerity of manner" and Philibert de la Mare noted of this lifelong bachelor that the "chastest girl never had such propriety"; cf. Henri Chevreul, *Hubert Languet* (1852; reprinted Nieuwkoop: B. De Graaf, 1967), pp. 172–173; Eugene and Emile Haag, *La France Protestante* (Paris, 1846–1859), 6:272.

[18]Having discussed the central issue of Nature and Art, beast and Man, we may presently mention the attempt of two critics to read the fable in ignorance of this issue, that is, as a topical historical allegory.

Ephim Fogel, "The Personal References in the Fiction and Poetry of Sir Philip

Better, then, be reconciled to Man's duplicity. The experience of reading the fable mirrors this duplicity, for the text invites two readings at once rather than a single one. But to elaborate two possibilities is not necessarily to endorse each of them equally. The reader must realize that he has a stake in choosing correctly because in choosing he will define not only the poem on the page but also himself:

He is a beast, that beaste's use will allowe[19] (4:70).

That the reader can choose at all indicates his potential difference from the beasts, but he does not realize that difference, become Man, until he chooses correctly.

Sidney" (Ph.D. dissertation, Ohio State University, 1958), pp. 104-23, claims that the fable, written in 1579, addresses the question of Anjou's marriage to Elizabeth. The tyrant Man represents Anjou; his depredations describe what will happen to England should Elizabeth accept him. (In *Terug naar de taekomst* [Leiden, 1971], pp. 7-16, J. A. van Dorsten apparently suggests a similar interpretation of the fable as a topical allegory addressed to 1579. I have not been able to find this work.) This view does not bear scrutiny. Why compromise such a warning against Anjou, whom Sidney evidently despized, with the concluding exhortation to patience? And why assign such a warning to Languet? Fogel's suggestion that Languet shared Sidney's hatred of Anjou is without foundation: on the contrary, as a supporter of Anjou, he strove to mitigate the effects of Sidney's opposition to the marriage scheme and attempted to coax him into Anjou's camp in the Low Countries (cf. Ch. 2, n. 21). Further, the fable represents Man's ascendancy over the beasts as an accomplished if problematic fact rather than as a prospective warning. But most of all, such an interpretation ignores the fable's informing dialectic of primitivism versus progress, its sure focus on the generalized issue of the origin and legitimacy of political sovereignty, and its pervasive and finely tuned use of irony as a means of dealing with this issue, including the systematic use of esthetic distance between speaker and author. To read this text as a topical historical allegory is to trivialize it.

[19]This is Geron, in the First Eclogues of *Old Arcadia*. He is censuring Philisides for using, in an earlier poem, a couple of metaphors derived from bestial behavior (4:70), although he will shortly reel off a spectacular string of such metaphors himself (4:74). I shall not discuss the logic of such incidental beast-wit, beyond noting that Geron's contradictory attitude to the propriety of such wit works on the same dialectical axis as does the fable (which examines the legitimacy of mapping from bestial "policy" into human) and that were Geron to bear in mind his own admonition —

He is a beast, that beaste's use will allowe,
For proofe of man, who spronge of heav'nly fire
Hathe strongest soule, when most his raynes do bowe

— when listening to Philisides' fable, he would have the wherewithal to make perfect sense of it.

CHAPTER SIX

Conclusion

In the beginning was a crime — Hannah Arendt

IN EVALUATING SIDNEY'S RELATION to the radical activists including Hotman, Buchanan, Beza, and Languet, we must distinguish between what the Germans call *Ausenpolitik* and *Innenpolitik*. In the domain of *Ausenpolitik* or foreign affairs, Sidney was sympathetic to the radical bloc and indeed active in its cause; witness his embassy to the German princes in 1577 and his acceptance of the Low Countries commission in 1585 and subsequent martyrdom. Indeed, his scheme to mount a maritime expedition with Sir Francis Drake which would battle Spain all the way to the New World displays the authentic note of Protestant imperialism. "Calviniser le monde" — Sidney's plans in this direction may have been little less relentless than those of his allies.[1]

However, in the realm of *Innenpolitik* or of the state's internal makeup, a different relation obtains. Sidney demurred from the desire of his French allies to carry into constitutional theory the Protestant emphasis on the original, unspoiled, or underivative condition. In addition, monarchomach theory betrayed a dependence on classical political models and idioms which Sidney considered "[matters] more in imaginacion than practice." Such models did not take into account the peculiar configuration of the nation state as it had evolved in the sixteenth century. This state predicated

---

[1] For the scheme with Drake and similar efforts, cf. Fulke Greville's *Life of Sir Philip Sidney* (Oxford: Clarendon Press, 1907), pp. 70–78, 109–20. The French phrase comes from a Calvinist quoted in Donald M. Kelley's *François Hotman: A Revolutionary's Ordeal* (Princeton: Princeton University Press, 1973).

a far more aggressively centralized executive than any of the classical masters knew, and Sidney regarded a weakened executive function with a trepidation equal to Shakespeare's. This position is compatible with that of Richard Hooker, who similarly rejected the Aristotelian dichotomy between centralized rule and law. In this view, centralized rule rather than confounding law guarantees it.

The irony of rejecting Protestant *Innenpolitik* while pursuing its foreign policy did not escape Sidney. He himself was careful to distinguish these two realms since he knew what difficulties attended their confusion. As his brother Robert reported in 1580, he drew a distinction between civil war, which he regarded as evil, and international war, which was not necessarily so.[2] This explains his refusal to join Anjou in 1576 and casts light on his reluctance to join Languet and Orange in 1580. (It is important to notice that when he did cross the channel in 1585, he went as a servant of Elizabeth, who had finally decided to declare publicly for Orange. The war he entered could thus no longer be construed as civil.) He played, I think, on a similar distinction in Book Two of the *New Arcadia*. This is the book that features Pyrocles and Musidorus' expedition through Asia Minor (the traditional haunt, ever since Herodotus, of tyrants) to aid several communities oppressed by evil rulers. Their rescue of the people of Pontus and Phrygia has been taken to indicate monarchomach sympathies.[3] But the inevitable dialectical rejoinder is that Sidney's heroes are not rebelling against their own monarchs but intervening as interested non-nationals: even Jean Bodin, the arch-foe of the monarchomachs, allowed and encouraged intervention against *foreign* tyrants.[4]

[2]

To note that Sidney rejected the Protestant *Innenpolitik* is by no means to cast him as a renegade absolutist. He no more deserves that label than Richard Hooker or Jean Bodin. What he rejected in the

---

[2]So Robert reported in a letter of November 1, 1580 to Sir Henry Sidney (Collins, *Letters and Memorials of State*[1746], quoted in Dorothy Connell, *Sir Philip Sidney: The Maker's Mind* [Oxford: Clarendon Press, 1977], p. 100).

[3]W.D. Briggs, "Political Ideas in Sidney's *Arcadia*," *SP* 28 (1931), 144–147; Martin Bergbusch, "Political Thought and Conduct in Sidney's *Arcadia*" (Ph.D. dissertation, Cornell University, 1971), pp. 245–248.

[4]Jean Bodin, *La République* 2.5.

monarchomachs was their uncompromising rationalistic attitude, not any and all systems of limitation on royal prerogative. Like Politique contemporaries, he felt that parliaments—such as the English one of which he was for several years a member—should have consultative rather than legislative rights. This position of moderate absolutism, known to the French as *monarchie tempérée*, does not have an accepted name in English; but it should clearly be distinguished from the theory of the mixed state, a term which should be reserved for the classical model and which generally does not transcend the notion of a balance or equal admixture of elements no single one of which predominates. Although I agree with Robertson, the latest editor of *Arcadia*, that Sidney's political theory may be likened to that of such contemporaries as Sir Thomas Smith, this should not be denominated a "mixed state" theory, insofar as Smith, like Sidney, was anxious to distinguish his view from that appropriate to the classical model.[5]

Not only were such models ill fitted to the "present case" of sixteenth century monarchy; Sidney went further and argued that in and of themselves they were unstable. Classical political "ideology," to use the modern term, for all the talk of mixture, was ultimately aristocratic. Like Hooker and Grotius, Sidney discerned a sophism in the classical argument for the "natural" superiority of optimates to commoners, and in such recipes as the Venetian and Spartan, a system for releasing the "greater" to organized plunder of the "lesser."

[5]Cf. Jean Robertson (ed.), *The Countess of Pembroke's Arcadia (The Old Arcadia)* (Oxford: Clarendon Press, 1973), p. xxviii, and cf. Sir Thomas Smith's disavowal of the weakened executive characteristic of the mixed state: in foreign affairs and diplomacy at least "the Kingdome of England is far more absolute than the Dukedome of Venice is, or the Kingdome of the Lacedemonians was" (*The Commonwealth of England* [1583], p. 44). Many English Renaissance jurists and statesmen saw no contradiction between moderately absolute rule and freedom. Thus, for example, Richard Bancroft speaks of the "freest and most absolute monarchies" (*Daungerous Positions and Proceedings* [1593] 1.6); Sir Walter Raleigh claims that Philip II "attempted to make himself not only an absolute monarch, like unto the kings of England and France, but Turk like, to tread under his feet all their natural and fundamental laws, privileges, and ancient rights" (*History of the World* [1614], Preface); and even Sir Edward Coke proves to his satisfaction that the "Kingdom of England is an absolute monarchy, and that the King is the only supreme governor as well over ecclesiastical persons, and in ecclesiastical causes, as temporal within this realm." I cull these examples from C. H. McIlwain, *Constitutionalism Ancient and Modern* (rev. ed., Ithaca: Cornell University Press, 1947), p. 147. Bodin terms England an absolute monarchy, adding that he derives this view from the civilian lawyer Valentine Dale, then English ambassador to France (*La République* 1.8). As in Bodin, the term "absolute" in the English writers does not imply the entire absence of legal limitations.

Even more blatantly oriented to the nobility were the monarchomachs. Rebellion, and freedom generally, were privileges of the
pars valentior. Ironically, since Sidney has made his reputation as a
symbol of the Elizabethan gentleman, the crux of his objection to the
monarchomachs lay in their attempt to rationalize the dominion of
the nobility. With due respect to his reputation, I know of few Renaissance authors more skeptical toward an exclusively aristocratic
bias. Though himself a member of the warrior aristocracy, he regarded its cult of martial "courage" with the utmost suspicion, and
his skeptical attitude toward this cult generates much of the ironic
energy of *Arcadia*.

Here is the real interest of Sidney's fable, and not the question of
rebellion, which may be viewed as subsidiary. It poises a state of
Nature where the "greater" command the "lesser" against a state of
Art wherein both have been subjected to a single ruler. This
amounts to more, I think, than the simple substitution of monarchic
"ideology" for aristocratic. Sidney's lesson can be generalized beyond sixteenth century circumstances.

Hannah Arendt can help to point this lesson as well as to explain
why modern readers have regularly had difficulty with Sidney's fable. Faithful children of the libertarian emphasis on origins, we have
tended to prefer the Natural or original condition in the fable to the
Artificial, derived, or eventual one. Sidney's view, according to
which Man's political maturity depends on his transcending the
primal state, goes against the modern grain. It nonetheless has a
name. In his defense of Art against Nature, progressivism against
primitivism, Sidney adhered, as Arendt can explain, to the Greek
notion of isonomy, or what we may call derived or conditional
equality:

> Isonomy guaranteed *isotēs*, equality, but not because all men were
> born or created equal, but, on the contrary, because men were by
> nature (*physei*) not equal, and needed an artificial institution, the
> polis, which by virtue of its *nomos* would make them equal. . . . The
> difference between this ancient concept of equality and our notion
> that men are born or created equal and become unequal by virtue
> of social or political, that is man-made institutions, can hardly be
> overemphasized.[6]

[6]Hannah Arendt, *On Revolution* (New York: Viking Press, 1963), p. 23. Cf. Hannah
Arendt, *The Human Condition* (Chicago: University of Chicago Press, 1958), p. 215:
"The equality attending the public realm is necessarily an equality of unequals who

Given the crucial proviso that he did not consider the classical city-state an effective means of securing equity, Sidney's concept of isonomy is the Greek one. In terms of Philisides' fable, the unregenerate condition features a nest of unequals, and equity is secured only by subordinating these unequals to an artificial or derived agency. Prior to the accession of the monarch, sheer force decided: once we disembarrass ourselves of Philisides' sentimental tendency to project human qualities onto beasts, we perceive instantly that the original condition is a Thrasymachean nightmare, with *stronger* animals ("Tygers, leopards, beares, and Lions' seed" [1. 122)] exercising dominion over the "*weaker* sort" (1. 121). Force — for what else is the domination of the weaker by the stronger? — decided until Man subjected all members of the community, both greater and lesser, to the same standard. Sixteenth century Politique theorists argued for a similar subjugation of all classes to centralized monarchy.[7] The point here — that men are *by nature unequal* — is precisely that of Sidney's Laconian episode as well. So long as it does not choose submission to a single extrinsic authority, the Laconian population will inevitably dissociate into two orders — gentlemen and Helots — who will consume each other in intestine warfare. Equity is secured not by attempting to melt these two orders into one, for the distinction is very real and cannot be abolished by mere fiat ("all distinction of names between gentleman and peasant to be quite taken away"), but rather by referring both orders to an authority extrinsic to each of them. Extrinsic in the sense that such an authority has no natural or aboriginal justification, and the attempt to rationalize it entirely or to locate such a justification is hopeless. All that primal Nature exhibits is the rude dominion of weaker by stronger — Philisides is never more reprehensibly fatuous than when he terms the physically more powerful the "nobler" (1. 121) — which habit of dominion to be broken calls for an answering vio-

---

stand in need of being "equalized" in certain respects and for specific purposes. As such the equalizing factor arises not from human "nature" but from outside. . . ."

[7] Cf. W. F. Church, *Constitutional Thought in Sixteenth Century France* (1941; reprinted, New York: Octagon Books, 1969), p. 139: "Perhaps the most far-reaching alteration of constitutional thought in the sixteenth century was the transition from the medieval conception of the social organism as composed of a great complex of individuals of varying rights, status, and consequent position in the hierarchical structure, to a theory wherein the people, if continuing to possess unequal rights and privileges as individuals, were reduced substantially to a great body of subjects alike in their subordination to the monarch."

lence. But once only. In the beginning of the state, as Arendt puts it, was a crime — but such a crime as strewed the way for equity. To guarantee this equity, the monarch must call on Art. Thus Euarchus must *"engraft"* singular confidence, the point of the horticultural metaphor being that such confidence does not obtain Naturally. The kind of equality he guarantees for his citizens is always a conditional one and pertains only to their public or political identity, since in regard to private station a craftsman will never equal a Dudley. The sovereign monarch, whom Sidney considers both "law give[r], and law rule[r]" (2:194), cannot abolish the natural distinction between "greater" and lesser," but he can mediate it.* Where the monarchomachs, all men of noble stock who were employees of nobles, sought to reinforce and make absolute the distinction between the nobility and the commoners, Sidney sought to mediate it and defined the "whole Arte of government" (1:187) accordingly.

Thus Sidney's ideal no less than that of the monarchomachs deserves to be called constitutionalist. This is the constitutionalism of the French Politiques and of Hooker. As we saw, these thinkers like Sidney repudiated the *Vindiciae* and similar works by developing a theory of unilateral donation of power — juridical analog to the primal crime. Properly subdued to the royal focus, the nobility has a positive role to play in such a state. But should a nobleman fall out with his ruler, he has no means of institutionalizing his dissatisfaction — he speaks as an individual. When Philanax, "lover of the king," recognizes that Basilius is erring, he tells him so, but he has no authority beyond that of the isolated reasoning voice. Compare *Gorboduc*, where the nobility at its centrifugal worst nearly destroys the state, but at its centripetal and consulatative best attempts to maintain its integrity.

Philanax is, if you like, the normative voice of *Arcadia*; that he is also a member of the aristocracy rather than a commoner measures Sidney's distance from our own age. The poet was sufficiently of his

---

*The famous tennis-court confrontation between Sidney and the Earl of Oxford testifies to Sidney's willingness to beard the "greater" in the name of a standard transcending private station. While Elizabeth saw fit to remind Sidney that he and Oxford were of different rank and that inferiors owe respect to their superiors, it is clear that Sidney was not prepared to accept the argument from private station as an absolute. By ordering that a duel be avoided, Elizabeth herself demonstrated the precedence of the political order to the feudal and private one.

century to feel that the "greater" such as Demagoras and Cecropia generally err by being subversive, whereas the "lesser" such as Dametas generally err by being buffoons. By insisting, however, that a Demagoras and a Dametas ultimately walk the same ground and owe allegiance to the same ruler, Sidney may have momentarily escaped his age — or at least that aspect of it that reflexly invoked the "chain of being" as a universal solvent for social problems.

[3]

Which of these two conceptions of politics — one, that of the monarchomachs, discerning a principle of order naturally or intrinsically within social stratification; the other, Sidney's, fetching a coercive principle from beyond the present class structure — represents a more responsible political attitude, the reader is invited to decide for himself. Let the reader decide, in addition, which of these two conceptions best deserves the modern tag of "conservative": that which depreciates the facile rationalizations of dominion and rejects the isomorphism between class structure and politics, or that which tautologously appoints the "greater" to be rulers and guardians of the "lesser."

Finally, the supreme irony of Sidney's life: his sovereign shared with many of the poet's modern students the conviction that he was a "king-fighter" at heart, and for this reason cut him off from active power. Sidney's ties to the continental Calvinists and his enthusiasm for a radical foreign policy were simply too much for the latitudinarian Elizabeth, even though few of her courtiers could have reasoned out as sedulously as did Sidney the logic of such centralized rule as she represented or been more skeptical toward mere political "courage." "I understand I am called very ambitious and proud at home," Sidney wrote several months before his death, "but if they knew my heart they woold not altogether so judg me" (3:167). For losing a capable, willing servant, Elizabeth had mainly her own gross misconception to blame.

This ends my study of Sidney's literary politics. I have not attended to every episode of political significance in Sidney's work, for such an enterprise would be interminable. I have focussed on those that seem to me to be most in need of clarification. I have not found it possible or necessary to provide an exact chronology of Sidney's political maturation or to demonstrate a single moment when he first began to doubt the rhetoric of the king-fighters, the important point here being that despite his years of tutelage in their care (1572–1575), Sidney came to his mature estimate of the Protestant *Innenpolitik* before writing a page of the *Old Arcadia*. And apart from adducing the crucial question of Nature and Art, a question that unifies everything Sidney ever wrote, I have not sought to integrate his political attitude with those that organize *Astrophil and Stella* or the great *Apology for Poetry*. What I have done is provide the groundwork for such a synthesis. The interested reader, fortified with the Nature and Art of Sidney's politics, is invited to pursue such a synthesis himself.

Appendices

Hubert Languet's Authorship of the
Vindiciae contra tyrannos

IN THIS ESSAY I shall suggest that it was Hubert Languet, working alone, who wrote and caused to be published under a pseudonym in 1579 the notorious Calvinist political treatise *Vindiciae contra tyrannos*. Only recently has this view, which was the accepted one from the mid-seventeenth century to the end of the nineteenth, been seriously revived. Elucidating the case for Languet's sole authorship involves excluding the other principal candidate, Philippe du Plessis-Mornay, from even a partial contribution to the work.[1] As I hope to show, in the years that saw the genesis and publication of the *Vindiciae*, Mornay's political views came near to being the opposite of those propounded in the treatise. All the same, Mornay's name could not have insinuated itself into this question without any reason at all. In fact Mornay insinuated it himself, suggesting to several intimates, decades after the publication of the work and of Languet's death, that he had had something to do with the *Vindiciae*. But the

---

[1]The reasoned case for Languet's authorship of the *Vindiciae*, which goes back to Pierre Bayle's "Dissertation concernant le livre d'Etienne Junius Brutus" in his *Dictionnaire historique et critique* (1692), generally prevailed until M. Lossen, "Uber die Vindiciae contra tyrannos des angeblichen Stephanus Junius Brutus," *Sitzungberichte der bayerische Akademie der Wissenschaften zu Munchen* 1 (1887), 215–54; A. Waddington, "L'auteur des *Vindiciae contra tyrannos*," *Revue Historique* 51 (1893), 65–69; and A. Elkan, *Die Publizistik der Bartholomausnacht und Mornays Vindiciae contra tyrannos* (Heidelberg, 1905), devised a case for Philippe du Plessis-Mornay. From Elkan's 1905 work until recently, few scholars apart from Ernest Barker, "The Authorship of the *Vindiciae contra tyrannos*," *Cambridge Historical Journal* 3 (1930), 164–181, affirmed Languet's sole authorship, although van Ysselsteyn's theory of Languet and Mornay's dual authorship proved acceptable to many (cf. G. T. van Ysselsteyn, "L'auteur de

evidence seems to me to confirm Ernest Barker's reluctant conclusion that Mornay's claim to the work was not actuated by the truth.[2] I shall speculate about what did actuate it, although this is a subsidiary question.

My brief for Languet will not satisfy those who need the smoking gun. Eventually, perhaps, it will turn up: an archive or an attic in Regensburg, or in Vienna, or in Prague, will yield his signed confession (his holograph manuscript, which was extant in the seventeenth century, would do just as well). But do we really need to wait for such a document? It seems to me that we have more than enough evidence to draw the proper conclusion.

[1]

The title page and prefatory apparatus of the *Vindiciae* may hide more than they reveal. The publication at Edinburgh is a fiction, since we know the work was published in Basle, and the pseudonymous "Stephano Junio Bruto Celta, auctore" does not seem to help (although the Scottish and "Celtic" allusions, perhaps a nod in the direction of Languet's friend George Buchanan, may be significant, and we shall return to the "Stephanus" component later). The 1579 date of publication, however, is correct, and I see no reason to doubt, at least in general outline, the account in the work's Preface, signed by an obviously fictional "Cono Superantius Vasco" and dated January 1, 1577 from Soleure, Switzerland. For all the indications are that the work was not composed in 1579, but rather

---

l'ouvrage *Vindiciae contra tyrannos*," *Revue Historique* 167 [1931], 46–59). Recently, however, Salvo Mastellone revived the case for Languet's sole hand in "Aspetti del'antimachiavellismo in Francia: Gentillet e Languet," *Pensiero Politico* 2(1969), 376–415. Further, I am delighted to note that the most recent examination of the authorship question, that of Henri Weber, decides for Languet: see Etienne Junius Brutus, *Vindiciae contra tyrannos: Traduction française de 1581*, ed. A. Jouanna, J. Perrin, M. Soulié, and A. Tournon; H. Weber, coordinateur (Geneva: Droz, 1979), pp. i–v. This critical edition appeared long after I had completed my own essay. While Weber et al. converge with me on the main issue of Languet's authorship, we disagree on certain subsidiary matters, for example, the party responsible for the Preface to the *Vindiciae*. I do not find tenable an attempt to suggest a third candidate apart from Languet or Mornay (Derek Visser, "Junius: The Author of the *Vindiciae contra tyrannos?*," *Tijdschrift voor Geschiedenis* 84 [1971], 510–25).
[2]Cf. Barker, op. cit.

several years earlier, and that the date of the Preface provides a reliable *terminus ad quem* for the period of composition.

Indeed there is little argument that Junius Brutus wrote the work roughly in the period of the fifth French civil wars (1574–1576), although he calculatingly omitted all but two or three direct allusions to current events or rulers; he mentions Henry III, who inherited the French throne in 1574, and seems to refer to the Emperor Maximilian II, who died in late 1576, as alive.[3] Salvo Mastellone's contribution is to tie the *Vindiciae* to one of the central events of the fifth wars — the combined Huguenot-Malcontent revolt against Henry III led by the king's younger brother, François d'Anjou et d'Alençon. He points out several passages in the work that acquire definition as cryptic references to Anjou (e.g., the reference to younger brothers of kings as proper inheritors of the throne). Further, he notes that Languet watched Anjou's revolt with great interest from his Vienna post in late 1575, met with Anjou's delegate in February 1576, was discussing at this time matters that turn up in the *Vindiciae* (e.g., the Polish election question), and quit Vienna in January 1577 with the intention of moving to France at the invitation (he surmises) of Anjou, to whom Languet intended to present the now complete *Vindiciae*.[4]

I should make two observations about Mastellone's construction of the case. First, his view of the *Vindiciae* as oriented to the 1575–1576 rebellion against Henry III should not be controversial, since it is implicit in the traditional assignment to the fifth wars and would be accepted even by Mornay's supporters such as Lossen. However, his view of the *Vindiciae* as Anjou's umbrella exclusively may prove misleading because the rebellion against Henry III was an international affair, involving, for example, German troops led by Prince John Casimir, for which Anjou served merely as the cutting edge, as the justificatory "subaltern magistrate." Indeed one of the most salient qualities of the *Vindiciae*, as opposed to the other monar-

---

[3]Unless otherwise noted, references shall be to the English translation: Hubert Languet, *A Defence of Liberty Against Tyrants*, a trans. of the *Vindiciae contra tyrannos*, introd. H. L. Laski (1924: reprinted, Gloucester, Mass.: Peter Smith, 1963). For Henry III, cf. p. 177. As for the reference to Maximilian II, this 1648 English translation omits it in favor of a more topical one to Ferdinand II; contrast *A Defence of Liberty*, pp. 160–161, with the original ed. of the *Vindiciae*, p. 137.

[4]Cf. Mastellone, op. cit.

chomach works, is its international aspect: the fourth and last
"Quaestio" argues for foreign intervention in a country oppressed
by tyranny, and several references acquire meaning in the light of
the multinational dynamics of the revolt against Henry III. Thus the
work's concluding historical exemplum notes that in 858 the Ger-
manic King Louis was persuaded by the oppressed French nobility
to invade their country to rescue it from the tyranny of his half-
brother Charles the Bald. This is clearly an allusion to the contemporary situation of the fifth wars, which saw the dissident French
nobility prevail with the German John Casimir to mount an invasion
of their country to rescue it from the tyranny (so they claimed) of
Anjou's older brother.[5] If the immediate locus of the *Vindiciae* was
France, the energies involved were pan-Protestant. Once this is
seen, however, the case for Languet's hand becomes stronger than
ever, and it no longer becomes necessary to suggest that Languet
wrote with Anjou in mind exclusively.

For Hubert Languet's involvement with the radical Protestant
bloc had an international aspect, with connections as deep to the
German princes as to his native France. Early in his career he wrote
William of Orange's 1562 *Justification* against Spain; by 1573 he was
in the employ of the Elector Augustus of Saxony (before that ruler's
renunciation of the radical cause); in 1575 and 1576 he fell out with
Augustus' advisers, who now turning to Lutheranism viewed him as
excessively radical; in 1579 he went to England in the train of John
Casimir, the most militant of the German princes, who had led the
German army into France in 1575; in 1579 and 1580 he served
William of Orange once again; and in 1580 he secretly mediated the
final agreement securing Anjou's sovereignty of the Low Countries
and had a hand in Orange's *Protestation* against Philip II. From beginning to end, then, he was intimately associated with the same
pan-European radical movement in the interests of which the *Vindiciae* was written and published.

In light of that work's composition in 1575–1576, Languet's falling
out with Augustus' advisers at this time, when they were purging
Saxon ranks of activist Calvinists, seems particularly significant. The
precise reason for the falling out remains obscure, although it is
certain that more than religion is involved in what historians some-

[5]Cf. Languet, p. 228.

times call the "Eucharist split." During the Regensberg diet of
November 1575, for example, the Elector Augustus was "showing
the most vehement indignation towards" Languet and his
coreligionists not only because of their doctrine of the Eucharist but
also because of their political activism including the impending invasion of France.[6] The Lutheran cabal at the Saxon court later
charged that Languet had interfered in the Polish election
question — one of the prime topics of the Regensberg diet — on behalf of some French candidate unacceptable to them (surely François d'Anjou, who having weeks earlier escaped from house arrest
and launched his revolt was regarded by the Calvinists as a happy
choice for the vacant Polish throne). The Lutherans kept pressing
similar politically based charges through 1576.[7] It is surely no accident that these indications of activism on Languet's part coincide
with the composition of the *Vindiciae*. As Languet continued his
prosecution of the radical cause — by the autumn of 1576 even
frankly championing the militants in his dispatches to his increasingly conservative patron[8] — a rift with Augustus became inevitable.

The Preface casts additional light on the work's genesis. Although
its author, Cono Superantius Vasco, is obviously pseudonymous, it
seems to me that we should take his account seriously and further
that a likely candidate exists for his true identity. He tells us that two
years prior to composing the Preface on January 1, 1577, he was
discussing "les misères de la France" (I quote now from the French
translation) with Junius Brutus; that the two of them decided it was
the acceptance by the French rulers of the pernicious doctrines of
Machiavelli that was responsible for the civil wars; that Junius
Brutus resolved to draft a godfearing answer to the impious Floren-
tine; that this answer was the *Vindiciae*, the completed manuscript of
which Junius Brutus delivered at some later date ("Depuis") to

---

[6]Cf. a letter of Zacharias Ursinus to Philip Sidney, November 5, 1575, recently
discovered and published by James Osborn, *Young Philip Sidney* (New Haven: Yale
University Press, 1972), pp. 380–382.
[7]Cf. Eugene and Emile Haag, *La France Protestante* (Paris, 1846–1859) 6:268, as well
as Languet to Augustus of Saxony, January 9, 1577, in *Arcana seculi decimi sexti. Huberti
Langueti legati, dum viveret, et consiliarii saxonici Epistolae secretae ad principem suum
Augustum Saxoniae ducem* (Halle, 1699). These letters will be identified by date only.
[8]Cf. Languet to Augustus, October 27, 1576: "Tot fraudibus et tanta perfidia sunt
superioribus annis usi ii, qui Regnum Gallicum administrant, ut videantur mihi stulte
facere ii, qui fidem ipsis habent: Quare, recte facient Huguenoti, si sibi caverint
quocunque praetextu milites illi conscribantur."

"Cono," "afin que je le leusse, pour puis apres luy en dire mon avis."[9]
Now precisely two years prior to the date of the Preface, or in
December-January of 1575, Hubert Languet was discussing contemporary affairs with his friend Henri Estienne, the printer-
humanist who was of a radical political affiliation;[10] Estienne was
again in Languet's company in mid-1576;[11] Estienne displayed as
rabid an antimachiavelism as that of the prefator;[12] and, finally, his
involvement in the *Vindiciae* would explain a fact in need of
clarification — the pseudonym *Stephanus* (=Estienne) Junius Brutus.
Although other candidates for "Cono Superantius Vasco" have been
suggested, including Languet himself, none seems to me to have as
good a claim as Henri Estienne. It was Estienne, I propose, whose
discussion with Languet in the winter of 1574–1575 adumbrated the
work, who received the manuscript upon its completion in mid-1576
and reviewed it with its author, who harbored it while Languet

[9]From the French translation of 1581, *De la puissance légitime du prince sur le peuple, et
du peuple sur le prince*, unpaginated Preface. The English translation does not contain
the Preface.

[10]In 1578 Estienne dedicated his *Nizoliodidascalus* to Languet, recalling "me ante
annos aliquot Viennae Austriae tecum deambulantem" (sig. A2r°). That Viennese
ambulatio in all probability occurred in the winter of 1574–1575, since it was then that
Estienne met Sidney, who was living in Vienna in the same house with Languet from
September 1574 to February 1575 (cf. Osborn, *Young Philip Sidney*, pp. 233–278).
While Sidney's biographers have always dated his meeting Estienne to the poet's
earlier brief visit to Vienna in 1573, it can be proven that this meeting could not have
taken place until Sidney's more extended 1574–1575 visit. Estienne never visited
Vienna before late 1974, at which time he enjoyed a leisurely stay of some weeks which
ended with his return to Geneva by January 18, 1575 (cf. his preface to *Parodiae morales*
[1575] as well as *Henrici Stephani ad Joannem Cratonem a Craftheim Epistolae* [Bratislava,
1830], letter of January 18). It must have been in this period that Estienne had the
discussion with Languet alluded to in the *Nizoliodidascalus*. Whether their friendship
predates this period I don't know.

[11]Languet wrote to Augustus from Vienna on March 15, 1576:

Est hic Vir doctus & Industriosus, qui per multos annos magnis sumptibus &
maximo labore collegit magnam vim Graecorum & Latinorum librorum man-
uscriptorum. Collegit etiam aliquot veteres statuas aeneas & marmoreas, &
multa pulcherrima vetera numismata. Etiamsi ista sint ei charissima, quia
tamen habet uxorem & liberos, nec opibus valde abundat, dixit mihi se libenter
Vestrae Celsitudini omnia ista aequo pretio divinditurum, si eorum esset
cupida. Ait, aliquot Principes Pontificios voluisse ea ab ipso emere, sed se
vendere noluisse, quoniam habere se dicit libros, in quibus sunt quaedam,
quae ad oppugnandum eorum Religionum usui esse possent. Ego etiam peto a
Vestra Celsitudine, ut suam de hac re voluntatem significare dignetur, quo
possit ille suis rebus consulere.

This "Vir doctus & industriosus" fits the description of Henri Estienne, who "per
multos annos magnis sumptibus & maximo labore" had visited libraries all throughout Europe in search of manuscripts for his numerous editions of the classical writ-

waited impatiently for the proper moment to break with the increasingly hostile and suspicious Augustus of Saxony, and who eventually contributed the Preface — tasks for which Languet rewarded him with the word "Stephanus" on the title page. (Estienne's account in the Preface remains in certain respects a partial one, with the view of the work's genesis and the polemic against Machiavelli reflecting his perspective more than Languet's, for their conversations were by no means the work's sufficient cause, and any reader of the work knows it comprises something other than the "Anti-Machiavel" promised in the Preface.) Finally, the moment for the break arrived in January 1577. On the first, Estienne composed the Preface, and eight days later Languet submitted his petition of resignation, asking to be released from Augustus' service in order that he might travel to France, where he saw impending "matters that pertain to the ruin or well-being of the Christian world."[13] Languet added that his first stop would be Frankfurt's upcoming Book Fair, where, he noted cryptically, he had personal business of some consequence.[14] It was from Frankfurt, the center of the Protestant printing industry, that he would launch the *Vindiciae*.

---

ers; who possessed in addition to these manuscripts a number of ancient medals or coins he had received from Huldrich Fugger (cf. A. A. Renouard, *Annales de l'imprimerie des Estienne* [1843], p. 381); who had written and printed books, particularly his notorious *Apologie pour Hérodote*, that savaged Roman Catholicism; and who "had a wife and [five] children and was not of abundant means," as Languet has it; indeed he was in serious financial straits at this very moment (cf. his comments on this theme in the contemporaneous letters to Crato). Thus he may well have attempted to raise money by selling, through Languet, items from his manuscript and coin collection. This puts Estienne in Languet's company in the spring of 1576 during the composition of the *Vindiciae*. There are also indications that they both attended the funeral of Maximilian II in October of this year, by which time the *Vindiciae* was completed.

[12]Cf. particularly Henri Estienne, *Deux discours du nouveau langage françois italianizé* (1578) as well as his *Principum monitrix musa* (1590), which repeatedly attacks *The Prince* as, for example, "magister omnis regimis tyrannici" (p. 256). It is interesting that the latter work begins with an approving allusion to Junius Brutus, a name that may have been recalled to Estienne by the republication of the *Vindiciae* in 1589.

[13]Languet to Augustus, January 9, 1577. "Res graviores & quae magis ad salutem aut perniciem orbis Christiani pertinent iam moventur in Gallia, & Inferiore Germania, quam usquam in Europa."

[14]"Ad id accedit, quod necessitas cogit me interesse proximo mercatui Francofortensi; nisi velim rerum mearum magnam iacturam facere: Eo enim mea causa venturi sunt plures cum quibus est mihi negocium." To be exact, this "proximus mercatus Francofortensus" refers to the entire Spring Fair; but surely Languet's destination was that aspect of it known as the Book Fair, the famous semiannual convention that brought men of letters and publishers together from all over Europe. For an account of the Book Fair, see Henri Estienne, *Francofordiense Emporium* (Geneva, 1574).

The *Vindiciae* was ready for the world, then, in January 1577. Why was it not in fact published at this time? Its investment in the Huguenot-Malcontent alliance against Henri III provides the answer. The alignment between the Huguenots and Anjou's Malcontents, which had provided the primary impetus to the composition of the work (Anjou lending a Valois name, and therefore legitimacy, to the revolt), had suddenly collapsed. In the last days of 1576 Henry III and Catherine had managed to entice the mercurial Anjou away from the Huguenots, whom he had never much liked anyway.[15] What was Languet to do now that the most crucial of the "subaltern magistrates" to whom his work appealed had suddenly abandoned the Calvinists? Nonplussed and confused, he proceeded to Frankfurt and conferred there during April with the printers to whom he had expected to entrust his manuscript.[16] There seemed little point in releasing the *Vindiciae* at that moment. Every letter he wrote revealed his despair at the deteriorating situation in France.[17] Only the visit in May of Sidney, who was in Heidelberg heading the English delegation to the German princes, provided any solace. Languet could at least share his hopes — and his manuscript — with the young man whom he considered his protégé and the rising star of Protestantism:

> With old true tales he woont mine eares to fill,
> How sheepheards did of yore, how now they thrive,
> Spoiling their flocke, ere while twixt them they strive.

[15]Anjou had been pressured by Catherine to become reconciled with Henry III before the convocation of the Blois estates in December. In early November Henry issued letters patent announcing Anjou's reconciliation to the crown. On January 1, (ironically the date of the Preface of the *Vindiciae*), Agrippa d'Aubigné, after a daring entry into the Blois chateau, offered the leadership of the Calvinists to Anjou — who refused. The following day Anjou was advising the king to mount a war against the "heretics" and offering to lead it himself. Nonetheless, no one seemed to feel entirely sure of Anjou's allegiances even then. Nevers reports on a scheme of Catherine's to imprison him, and on January 24, the English ambassador reported that "the jalousye between the French King and Duke of Allenson was never greater." (Cf. d'Aubigné, *Histoire Universelle* [Paris, 1886–1909] 5:114–16; Louis de Gonzague, duc de Nevers, *Mémoires* [Paris, 1665] 1:179–288; *Calendar of State Papers, Foreign Series, of the Reign of Elizabeth*, January 1577.)

[16]Languet's letter of April 9 to the Camerarii, for example, adverts to business with Claude Marni, a printer in the establishment of his old friend Andreas Wechel; cf. *Viri clar. Huberti Langueti burgundi ad Joach. Camerarium patrem et Joach. Camerarium filium medicum, scriptae Epistolae* (Groningen, 1646), with letters to be cited by date only. Although I cannot unravel Languet's dealings at this time with the Camerarii, Marni, Wechel, and others, they would seem to repay further work.

[17]Cf. Languet to the Camerarii, March 1, April 9 ("De rebus Gallicis nihil nisi triste"), June 17 ("Nostris in Gallia omnia infoeliciter succedunt"), etc.

The low ebb of French affairs lent special poignancy to Languet's indictment, this spring, of shepherds' "spoiling their flock." The last straw came with the news in early summer that Anjou, having upon his desertion to the court been invested as field commander of the royal armies against the Huguenots, had slaughtered his former allies, first at La Charité and then at Issoire. Despite their disagreement on other issues, Sidney shared Languet's shock at Anjou's treachery, later recalling it to his queen in the famous "marriage letter" excoriating Anjou: "That [Anjou] himself contrary to his promise & against all gratefullnes, having had his liberty & principall estate cheefly by the Hugnotes meanes did sack La Charité & utterly spoiled Issoire with fire & sword" (3:52).[18] The central hope of the Calvinists having abandoned the cause, Languet now had no choice but to shelve his manuscript.

But if Anjou could desert the Huguenots, he could also return, and thus resume the role in which Languet's *Vindiciae* cast him. Even while the memory of his treachery was still warm, he began to connive with the Low Countries Protestants. As early as the Paix de Monsieur, William of Orange had sounded him out on the possibility of playing a role in the Low Countries. Orange's idea was to have Anjou assume the sovereignty of the southern provinces of Flanders and Brabant. Sure of the northern, predominantly Calvinist, provinces of Holland and Zeeland, Orange felt that Anjou could help him by holding the southern, predominantly Catholic, provinces out of the grip of Spain. Smelling a new chance to exercise power, Anjou pursued Orange's suggestion with delight; and soon a new alliance between Anjou and the Protestants was in the making.[19]

Now all are agreed that William of Orange's campaign against Spain in 1579 finally provided the occasion for the publication of the *Vindiciae*. Languet, who had gravitated from Augustus' service into that of Orange, played a key role in this campaign. Orange's chaplain, Loyseleur de Villiers, persuaded Languet to dust off the manuscript of the *Vindiciae* in 1579.[20] Now that Anjou was once again on the Calvinist side, the time was right. Languet made no changes in his text, the argument *contra tyrannos* being sufficiently generalized

---

[18]On La Charité, cf. Languet to the Camerarii, June 17, 1577.
[19]For the primary documents, cf. P. L. Muller and A. Diegerick, *Documents concernant les relations entre le duc d'Anjou et les Pays-Bas 1576–83* (Utrecht, 1889–1899).
[20]While I take issue with another facet of Grotius' testimony below, that involving the role of Loyseleur and Orange in the publication of the *Vindiciae* is generally accepted.

to apply to the Spanish usurpation in the Low Countries as well as to Henry III (although we have no trouble discerning the work's true orientation to the 1575–1576 invasion of France); he retained Estienne's two-year-old Preface (which of course is innocent of reference to the Low Countries); and he agreed to the addition of prefatory and postscriptory verses, perhaps by Philippe de Marnix (the only component of the work that may originate in the Low Countries).[21] Between May and September 1579 the otherwise regular correspondence of Languet and Sidney was halted while Languet saw his work through Thomas Guérin's press in Basle.[22] In October he attended the Cologne conference for the pacification of the Netherlands and discreetly let the first copies circulate: the *Acta* of this congress, compiled during the winter of 1579–1580 by Aggaeus Albada and published in 1580, is the first document to quote from the *Vindiciae*.[23] Then in 1580 Languet traveled to France and secretly mediated the final agreement securing Anjou's sovereignty of Flanders and Brabant (an episode testifying to the same blind faith in Anjou that had actuated him in 1575–1576) and arranged for a second edition of the *Vindiciae*.[24] It is significant that when Philippe

[21]The prefatory verses are signed "L. Scribonius Spinter, *Belga*," the postscriptory ones, "Alphonsus Menesius Benavides, Tarraconensis."

[22]The break in the correspondence was noted by Barker, p. 177. Just before the break, we find Languet once again at the Frankfurt Book Fair. For Guérin's printing the work, see below.

[23]It was Lossen who noticed the extensive quotations from the recently published *Vindiciae* in these *Acta*; cf. "Aggaeus Albada und der Kölner Pacificationscongress," *Historisches Taschenbuch* (1876), p. 358. This champion of Mornay would have done well to notice that it was Languet, and not Mornay, who attended the congress in question.

[24]On Languet's role in the 1580 delegation of Anjou, see: H. Chevreul, *Hubert Languet* (1852; reprinted Nieuwkoop: B. De Graaf, 1967), pp. 159–163; G. Groen van Prinsterer (ed.), *Archives ou correspondance inédite de la maison d'Orange-Nassau* (Leiden, 1837–1847), Utrecht, 1857–1861), 1st series, 7:335–337; Muller and Diegerick, *Documents* 3:320, 496; Kervyn de Lettenhove, *Les Huguenots et les gueux* (Brussels, 1883–1885) 5:550–558. Some years after Languet's death, Mornay stated flatly of the 1580 mission: "[Languet] avoit été employe particulièrement par Monsieur le Prince d'Orange vers Monsieur [Anjou], pour faire sa condition, & de sa maison avec lui, par laquelle il lui laissoit la Hollande & Zélande en propriété" (Mornay's note in J.-A. De Thou, *Histoire Universelle* [Basle, 1742] 6:147). The evidence of the aforementioned documents proves conclusively that the brothers Haag (6:270) are wrong to take at face value Languet's claim to Sidney on May 6, 1580 that he is traveling to France only for "some private matters [quasdam privatas . . . res]." On July 24, admitting his interviews with Anjou, Languet attempted to reassure Sidney, whose aversion to the French prince was familiar to him: "I have spoken with Anjou of many matters, and, if one may judge by his discourse, he seems disposed rather to docility than to pride and cruelty [potius propenso ad humanitatem quam ad crudelitatem]." The sympathy between Languet's role in mediating between Orange and Anjou and his authorship of the *Vindiciae* has not been remarked on previously.

de Marnix travelled to Plessis-lès-Tours in August 1580 to formalize the agreement with Anjou, he adduced ideas and exampla which appear in the *Vindiciae*.[25] At the end of the year Languet wrote or collaborated in William of Orange's *Apology* against Philip II, a work that has numerous well-known parallels to the *Vindiciae*. Languet's feeling that the Calvinist design was finally coming to crisis is reflected in his 1580 correspondence with Sidney, whom he urged, with a single-mindedness equal to that of the *Vindiciae*, to play the right Protestant part of action.[26]

It was also in 1580 — here is my modest contribution to the dossier of external evidence regarding the *Vindiciae* — that Sidney attached Languet's name to a fictional political essay that, regardless of its ultimate purpose, invites construction as an indictment *contra tyrannos*.* Indeed, by virtue of its composition in 1580, Sidney's text may claim to be the earliest reasoned analysis of the *Vindiciae*, the second of which I am aware occurring in Adam Blackwood's *Pro regibus apologia* of 1581. This text validates Mastellone's guess, made in ignorance of *Arcadia*, that the poet was among the first Englishman to acquire familiarity with the *Vindiciae*.[27]

Hubert Languet was a moral absolutist, one of the "terrible simplifiers" who somehow expected to use such paladins as John Casimir or François d'Anjou without soiling his own "cleane hands." Perhaps mercifully, then, he was spared by his death in 1581 from seeing the Calvinist design shattered once again by Anjou's treachery — this time, the "furie française" of 1583 whereby Anjou attempted to seize Antwerp from his own allies. Like many theocrats,

---

[25]Cf. Gordon Griffiths, "Humanists and Representative Government in the Sixteenth Century: Bodin, Marnix, and the Invitation to the Duke of Anjou to Become Ruler of the Low Countries," in *Representative Institutions in Theory and Practice* (Brussels: 1970), p. 70. My point is that Languet primed the formal embassy with his ideas on hedging sovereignty, the chief theme of the negotiations at Plessis-lès-Tours.

[26]See Languet to Sidney on January 30, March 12, May 6, September 24, and October 22, 1580.

[27]Cf. Mastellone, p. 404: "È possibile che sia stato il Sidney a far conoscere in Inghilterra prima del 1600 il testo delle *Vindiciae*."

*May I remind you that I am not constructing a circular argument. No matter what it tells us about Sidney, "Ister banke" has never been adduced by scholars concerned with the authorship of the *Vindiciae*. That Sidney, who was close both to Mornay and to Languet, should have chosen to implicate Languet in a story speaking of the rights of the community vis-à-vis tyrants, and this in 1580, strikes me as something that should be brought to the attention of students of the *Vindiciae*. But the use of this text as pertaining to the authorship question may be distinguished from its use as pertaining to Sidney's thought, and my study does not call for either one of these uses to depend on the other.

Languet remained constitutionally oblivious to the ambiguities of power, trusting that the cause would somehow automatically transcend the limitations inherent in its instruments.

[2]

If Languet was intimately involved with the radical bloc in the interests of which the Calvinists invaded France and published the *Vindiciae*, the case with Philippe du Plessis-Mornay, the alternative candidate, is otherwise.

Mornay was one of those Protestants who took a dim view of Anjou and the Malcontents. In 1573, he told La Noue, who was deliberating whether to throw in his lot with the Malcontents, "qu'il ne failloit point mesler les affaires de la Religion avec celles de monseigneur le duc d'Alençon, mais faire son cas a part et se contenter d'avoir bonne intelligence avec lui."[28] Although he joined the invasion force in October 1575 (indeed he was captured by the Guise army and held prisoner for ten days before escaping), he soon thereafter condemned the erratic and presumptuous nature of the Malcontent nobles in no uncertain terms and refused to rejoin them.[29] He later regularly reprimanded the Huguenots for trusting blindly in such an opportunist as Anjou.[30] His actions in 1576 are particularly significant. Though he maintained a nominal connection with Anjou, he broke it definitively when, at the end of the year, he saw the Valois prince begin to slide toward the court: "appercev-

[28]Mme de Mornay, *Mémoires* (Paris, 1868–69) 1:74.

[29]Mme de Mornay, 1:90–92, 94–101, 104–05. Significantly, Mornay also refused to join Condé's forces in December, for whose offer cf. L. Bastard d'Estang, *Vie de Jean de Ferrières* (Auxerre, 1858), pp. 257–263.

[30]Cf. Mme de Mornay, p. 105: "[The Huguenots] ne pouvaient pas penser que monseigneur le Duc peust jamais quitter nostre party, dont ilz furent trompés comme ilz le connurent tost apres. Et puis tesmoigner que jamais monsieur de Plessis n'en peut concevoir ny attendre autre chose." Cf. also p. 143 on the subject of Anjou's ultimate treachery in Antwerp in 1583: "Je luy ay souvent ouy dire, lorsqu'on parloit de la trahison d'Anvers, qu'il n'eut jamais joye plus profonde que quand il eu sceut l'yssue vengereuse d'une telle perfidie, et monseigneur le Prince d'Orange avouoit ordinairement qu'il luy avoit souvent prédit cela." On the same subject, cf. Mornay's "I told you so" to Orange on February 14, 1583: "Je crois que vostre excellence se sera resouvenue de moi a ce propos; car je craignois, lors que je partis, pis que je n'osois dire, et me sembloit que ne vous faisois plaisir de vous troubler la bonne opinion [i.e., of Anjou] que vous aviés." Mornay thanks God that he had the foresight to break with Anjou as early as he had — "j'ai loué Dieu mille fois de ce qu'on me reculoit de là." (Cf. Morray, *Mémoires et correspondance* [Paris, 1824–25] 2:225.)

ant son intention d'aller en court et quitter le party, il s'en démesla, prit congé de luy, declara franchement qu'il le voyait prendre un chemin auquel il ne pensoit pas le pouvoir servir selon son honneur et conscience."[31] He then immediately offered his services to Henry of Navarre, whose approach to the French throne was based on legitimacy rather than violent insurrection.

Further, in the course of 1576 Mornay wrote two lengthy remonstrances arguing for observance of the May peace rather than violent intervention. In these two works he took what may be described as a classic Politique attitude: to holy war should be preferred the mundane compromise of peace. Both remonstrances urge the coexistence of the two religions on the ground that this will best ensure the political stability of the realm. Civil war would irreparably damage the nation. France is already perilously divided, with the king restricted to the provinces immediately around Paris and all the provinces beyond the Loire in the hands of "ceulx de la religion prétendue réformée" (a reference that allows us to date this *Remonstrance aux etats de Blois* to the summer of 1576).[32] The situation has deteriorated to the point where "le moindre seigneur de ce royaume, voire un voleur publique" can find a band of armed men and "faire partie contre le roy."[33] Mornay has a nightmare vision of what happens when the "parti vitale" of the political organism, "qui est l'amour des sujets envers le prince," becomes ill: "Cest estat se résoudra comme un corps mort en serpens, en vers, en crapaux, en un million de bestes sans raison qui s'entremangeront les unes les autres, et feront trop plus de mal au peuple, que ne font tout ceulx dont il se plaint."[34] Significantly, he keeps hoping for focus and unity in the king, the same Henry III whom both Languet and the author of the *Vindiciae* regarded with contempt: "Tout ce royaume n'est qu'une cité, qu'une maison, qu'ung corps, qui n'a qu'un roy, un

---

[31]Cf. Mme de Mornay, 1:110–11.
[32]This Remonstrance is printed in Mornay, *Mémoires et correspondance*, 2:60–78. The quoted phrase, p. 73. In defense of the Paix de Monsieur, Mornay also wrote a *Remonstrance d'un bon Catholique françois aux trois estats de France* (s.l., 1576), for a description of which cf. B. L. O. Richter, "French Renaissance Pamphlets in the Newberry Library. I. The Debate between Philippe de Plessis-Mornay and Louis Dorléans," *Studi francesi*, fasc. 11 (1960), 220–240. While distinct from the other 1576 Remonstrance, this presents an identical argument. Further, Mornay personally assisted in the negotiations for the Paix (cf. Mme de Mornay 1:107).
[33]Mornay, *Mémoires et correspondance*, 2:71.
[34]Ibid., 2:74.

père de famille, ung chef."[35] He explicitly attacks the Malcontents as grasping, greedy figures who sacrifice national unity to personal advancement: they are a "race tres dangereuse" animated by "convoitise du gain et de vain honneur . . . , d'ung fol amour de soi-mesme."[36] This constitutes no less than diametrical opposition to the pro-rebellion, federalist, decentralizing stance of the *Vindiciae*, and an unambiguous attack on the same trigger-happy dissident nobles such as Thoré, Condé, Anjou, whose alliance with the Huguenots and invasion of France the monarchomachs regularly vindicated. It is also significant that Mornay, who seems to have deeply repented his own fleeting role in the invasion, should, here in the summer of 1576, have an eloquent condemnation of Casimir's German troops, who were now returning home laden with booty and leaving a terrorized peasantry in their wake.[37] Neither Languet, who served Casimir and considered himself more German than French, nor the author of the *Vindiciae*, who devoted an entire "Quaestio" to the legitimacy of foreign intervention, ever had any scruples about launching Germans onto French soil.[38] Finally, Mornay even explicitly analyzes and rejects the "inferior magistrate" theory of rebellion that is at the heart of the *Vindiciae*: "The malcontent . . . prefers the inferior to the superior, following for his own profit a prince or subaltern magistrate [ung prince, ou seigneur subalterne] against his king and rightful ruler."[39]

In urging that national unity be placed above sectarian difference and ambition, Mornay was a Politique in the classic sense of the word, one in the mold of Montaigne, Pasquier, and l'Hôpital. It seems inconceivable that Mornay, whose two 1576 remonstrances present a clear statement of Politique irenicism, should at the same time have written the *Vindiciae*.[40]

---

[35]Ibid., 2:73. In regard to Henry III, contrast Languet, p. 177, as well as many similarly contemptuous references scattered throughout Languet's correspondence (e.g., December 24, 1573 and February 5, 1574 to Sidney, January 9, 1577 to Augustus, etc).

[36]Mornay, 2:70.

[37]Ibid., 2:73.

[38]Readers of Languet's correspondence will appreciate the justness of this comment in the introduction to the 1646 volume of letters to the Camerarii: "Natione Gallus, sed animi candore, fide, cultu & moribus vere Germanus fuit" (sig. **10v°). Significantly, Languet's papers remained in Germany and it was at Groningen, Halle, and Frankfurt that his correspondence was published.

[39]Mornay, 2:70–71. Mornay's condemnation of the Huguenots throughout this work, or at least of the activist wing thereof, is quite remarkable.

[40]It is imperative to distinguish two references of the word "Politique." First, it indicates the conciliatory stance according to which national unity was to be placed

The fundamental inconsistency between Mornay's 1576 remonstrances and the *Vindiciae* was noted in passing by Barker but otherwise has not been adequately recognized.[41] Certainly Elkan, whose *Die Publizistik der Bartholomausnacht* (1905) remains the fullest brief for Mornay's authorship, did not cope with it. Elkan did not help his case by claiming as Mornay's an *Exhortation a la Paix aux catholiques françois* published in 1574 (an attribution accepted by Hauser, Patry, and myself).[42] This *Exhortation* has the same irenic approach as the 1576 remonstrances. Elkan attempted to suggest that this *Exhortation* together with the 1576 *Remonstrance aux etats de Blois* formed the basis of the *Vindiciae* but ended by admitting that the former writings differ from the *Vindiciae* both in tone and purpose.[43] He granted that Mornay "saw in the harmony between prince and people the greatest safeguard of the state, and every disruption of this harmony seemed to him highly dangerous."[44] Elkan could give no coherent explanation of how Mornay could be responsible both for his royalist writings of 1574–1576 and for the *Vindiciae*, beyond suggesting rather desperately that Beza's *Du droit des magistrats* (1574) may have convinced him of the justice of rebellion[45] — but

---

above sectarian religious differences. This was the position of such thinkers as Montaigne, Michel de l'Hôpital, La Noue, Etienne Pasquier, Pibrac, de Belloy, du Fay, Grégoire, and the author(s) of the *Satyre Ménipée*, for whom no religious dogma was worth the trauma of the civil wars. Unfortunately, the word "Politique" has also been used to refer to the historical party led by Anjou from 1573 until his death (e.g., by Francis De Crue, *Le Parti des Politiques au lendemain de la Saint-Barthélemy* [Paris, 1892]). Since this party depended on a combination of Huguenot and Catholic support, they regularly urged coexistence of the two religions. However, there is no necessary connection between the theoretical position called Politique and the party led by Anjou. In fact, that party diametrically opposed such a position, since under Anjou's tenure it was the party of armed revolt, whereas the theoretical position seeks to conciliate and include, and is almost by definition against armed revolt and legitimist. Cf. J. Neville Figgis, *Studies in Political Thought from Gerson to Grotius* (Cambridge: University Press, 1907), p. 110: "It was the very raison d'être of the Politiques, who for the most part proclaimed the duty of loyalty to a sovereign of a different religion, to proclaim the wisdom if not the duty of toleration, and to assert the notion of indefeasible hereditary right." To avoid confusion, I reserve the word Politique for the irenic position and call Anjou's party by a name many contemporaries including Mornay applied to them — the Malcontents.

[41] Barker, p. 178. However, his historical analysis is limited by confusion as to Anjou's role, whom he imagines to have stood for peace.

[42] Elkan, pp. 90–97; cf. H. Hauser, *Les Sources de l'histoire de France: seizième siècle (1494–1610)* (1906–15; reprinted, Nendeln, Lichtenstein: Kraus Reprint, 1967), no. 2259; and Raoul Patry, *Philippe Du Plessis-Mornay* (Paris: Fischbacher, 1933), pp. 272–275.

[43] Elkan, p. 105.

[44] Ibid., p. 95.

[45] Ibid., p. 96.

then even by his own reckoning Mornay's royalist attitude is evident well after this date.

Far from being localized to 1574–1576, Mornay's king- and peace-centered position was the great constant of his political thought. He reiterated it in the 1580s on several occasions in response to Guise pamphleteers who were now the chief purveyors of the monarchomach argument. Throughout these works the ardent pacifist and monarchist reasserted himself repeatedly.[46] Further, Mornay's lengthy *Vérité de la religion chrestienne* (1581) may be viewed as an attempt to give a philosophical underpinning to the Politique idea. As against the exclusivity and sectarianism of the monarchomach polemic, this work develops an inclusive and catholic argument according to which certain universally held "communes notions" such as the apprehension of God, the desire for immortality, and the hope of happiness provide the ground for political unity.[47] That Mornay should have served Henry IV faithfully for thirty-four years — the *Vérité* is dedicated to him — provides further eloquent testimony to his Politique ideals, since Henry's approach to the throne was based on legitimacy and his signature of the Edict of Nantes represents the triumph of the Politique idea in France. As Pierre Bayle long ago noted, no book could have been more pernicious to Henry of Navarre than the *Vindiciae*.[48] When in the difficult

---

[46]For these works, see Richter, pp. 226–228, who emphasizes their irenic nature. One of these, a 1586 *Exhortation et remonstrance*, is largely a *rifacimento* of Mornay's 1576 *Remonstrance aux etats de Blois*. Richter does not discuss the contradiction between Mornay's general theme and that of the *Vindiciae*, beyond noting: "It seems paradoxical that [Mornay's monarchomach opponent] Dorléans, had he looked for any learned theoretical structure to justify his call to rebellion, could have defected to the camp of the enemy and claim for himself large pieces of Mornay's *Vindiciae contra tyrannos* . . ." (p. 235–236). The paradox disappears, of course, once we disembarass Mornay of the *Vindiciae*.

[47]Mornay, *De la vérité de la religion chrestienne* (1581). Mornay's aim in this, his major philosophical work, is clearly irenic. Thus in the chapter seeking to show "Qu'il y a un seul Dieu," he develops the theme of unity in a political sense: "l'Ethique ou Philosophie morale, réduit en un mesme homme, plusieurs diverses passions à une raison: l'Oeconomique, réduit plusieurs hommes à l'obeissance d'un père de famille: la Politique plusieurs familles à une Cite, qui n'est que de plusieurs citoyens une unité, soit soubs une mesme loy, soit soubs la conduite d'un seul. . . . Tout ce donq, que l'homme conceit, invente & dispose, nous conduit toujours a l'unité: Ou l'unité se perd, les choses perissent, les arts se confondent [,] les républiques se dissolvent" (p. 35). Mornay's use of the notion of *prisca theologia* throughout this work also represents a strategy characteristic of Politique thinkers, as D. P. Walker shows in "The *Prisca Theologia* in France," *Journal of the Warburg and Courtauld Institutes* 17 (1954), 204–259, especially p. 258.

[48]Bayle, "Dissertation," p. 141: "Rien ne pouvait être plus pernicieux à Henri IV que le livre de Languet, parce qu'il autorisait les Français à déposer Henri III, et a conférer la couronne au duc de Guise." Not, of course, that the *Vindiciae* was written

years before assuming the throne Henry thought of taking up arms, Mornay replied that he did not consider this either just or necessary.[49] When Henry, once on the throne, began to find his monarchy threatened by the regional Protestant nobility, Mornay made efforts that were little short of heroic to mediate between the monarch and the dissidents. The closest student of Mornay's career in the 1590s remarks on the incongruity between his staunch irenicism and monarchism at this point and his putative authorship of the *Vindiciae*.[50] After Henry IV's assassination in 1610, Mornay continued to uphold the Politique position, supporting the throne against the provincial nobility, until his death in 1623. In a codicil to his will he warned his sons-in-law and grandchildren never to take part in political uprisings "which are plotted through the passion and selfishness of great lords, and which thus cause minds to trespass the borders of duty and conscience."[51] This was his theme for fifty years, and it was particularly his theme in 1576, the year in which the *Vindiciae*, which pursues the opposite idea, came to be.[52] Consistency may occasionally be a dubious virtue, but why invent inconsistencies where none exist? Mornay was consistently a Politique royalist and antipathetic to the Malcontents. Conversely, the Malcontents, upon whom the Calvinists relied to found their theocracy, had consistently the sympathy and service of Languet.

[3]

Computer-assisted stylistic arguments are notoriously prone to abuse. I find most dubious Jagger's recent argument for Mornay on

---

with the Guise in mind; but this did not hinder them from finding its arguments apposite.

[49]Mme de Mornay 1:128. Mornay did, however, help to raise funds for Navarre.

[50]Joseph A. Airo-Farulla, "The Political Opposition of the Huguenots to Henry IV, 1589 to 1598" (Ph.D. dissertation, University of Washington, 1969), pp. 53–54. Cf. pp. 15–16: "In spite of his opposition to the King's conversion, Du-Plessis Mornay never contemplated turning this disappointment into political opposition." Also p. 13: "In political matters [Mornay] was a moderate man, completely loyal to the king, ultimately seeing Henry as the only legitimate agent through which the welfare of Calvinism could be secured in France."

[51]Quoted by Lossen, pp. 235–36.

[52]While a good many Calvinists abruptly changed their tune to a conciliatory one in 1584 when Henry of Navarre displaced Anjou as heir apparent, Mornay's career displays no such self-serving reversal. He earned his right to speak for the Politique position by articulating it clearly years before it was fashionable or prudent for Protestants to do so.

the basis of statistical analysis of sentence length.[53] Jagger takes as his sample of Languet's prose style only a number of the letters to Sidney; as Lossen, an earlier supporter of Mornay, had occasion to recognize, a learned essay and a familiar epistle had entirely different stylistic parameters in the Renaissance; thus it is doubtful that a contrast in sentence length between Languet's letters (few of them at that) and the *Vindiciae* proves anything.[54] On the other hand, I do not despair of using some general arguments from tone and idiom as a way of adjudicating between Languet and Mornay. It seems to me that such evidence accuses Languet rather than Mornay.

The idiom of the *Vindiciae* is evidently legalistic. Unlike, say, George Buchanan, whose monarchomach *De jure regni* reveals broadly humanist sympathies (e.g., much quotation from Cicero, the humanist genre of the dialogue), Junius Brutus is most at home with the subtleties of Roman civil law, an influence on the *Vindiciae* that has recently been well studied.[55] Similarly, the disposition of arguments into questions of the *an sit* form ("an liceat resistere Principi") reveals a scholastic, disputatious cast of mind formed in a school of law rather than one raised in the newer humanist fashion. This points to Languet, trained in civil law, rather than to Mornay. Mornay's works suggest a broad, inclusive, scripturally based humanism, interested in reconciling Plato, Plotinus, and Seneca with the word of God, but devoid of the interest in legal texts and maneuvers that marks the *Vindiciae*. If Coleridge was right that everyone is either a Platonist or an Aristotelian, then Mornay was clearly an inclusive and even enthusiastic Platonist (cf. particularly the great *Vérité de la religion chrestienne*) whereas Junius Brutus and Languet were prim, dessicated Aristotelians.

The use of scripture in the *Vindiciae* is sometimes taken as indicating Mornay's authorship since he wrote theological works; but its scriptural aspect is regularly exaggerated. It is true that the *Vindiciae* has exampla from Old Testament history such as Moses' binding certain tribes beyond the Jordan to aid Israel against her enemies, but these were the stock examples from Huguenot polemic; almost

---

[53]Graham Jagger, "On the Authorship of the *Vindicioe contra tyrannos*," *Durham University Journal* n.s. 29 (1968), 73–80.

[54]Lossen, p. 221.

[55]Cf. William Freegard, "Roman Law and Resistance Right: A Study of Question Three of the *Vindiciae contra tyrannos*" (Ph.D. dissertation, University of Iowa, 1971).

every one of them could be found in Beza's *Du droit des magistrats*, upon which Junius Brutus relied heavily;[56] they certainly don't indicate anything like "a profound acquaintance with scripture."[57] The scripture is there to give a God-fearing flavor to the legal argument. Thus while van Ysselsteyn's distinction between a legalist Languet and a theological (I should have said inclusive or conciliatory) Mornay is acceptable and helpful, his use of this distinction to discover two different authors in the *Vindiciae* is not. He assigned Question Three, where Aristotle and civil law predominate, to Languet (this was already to concede much the largest and most important fraction of the work to Languet) and the much briefer Questions One, Two, and Four to Mornay on the ground that they contain more scriptural references than the third.[58] But it is not only Question Three that draws on Aristotle and civil law; it is in effect the entire tract. If Questions One and Two have more scriptural references than Three, this is because Junius Brutus needs scripture at the beginning of his work to bring Christians over to a thesis for which there is little room in the traditional Christian attitude: that armed rebellion is just (it would be well to remember that not all Protestants were willing to take up arms against the king). Thus Questions One and Two produce—not without a good deal of ingenuity— "pregnant testimonies drawn from holy writ" to the end that Junius Brutus "might take away all scruple regarding this question";[59] only then does Junius Brutus make the transition to the formal legal argument of Question Three. This transition is clearly planned and articulated as such by a single author; it is not something that results from patchwork. And even in the early Questions, if the exempla are scriptural, the idiom is legalistic: "And as two covenanters by promise, especially in contracts, the obligation whereof exposes the obligees to forfeitures, and hazards, such as this is here, the failings of the one endamages the other: so that if Israel forsake their God, and the king makes no account of it, he is justly guilty of Israel's delinquency."[60] It is the idiom (of contract, forfeiture, delinquency), rather than the perfunctory and tendentious use of the Old Testa-

---

[56]Cf. Julian H. Franklin (trans. and ed.) *Constitutionalism and Resistance in the Sixteenth Century* (New York: Pegasus, 1969), p. 39.

[57]Laski, in Languet, p. 59.

[58]van Ysselsteyn, op. cit.

[59]Languet, p. 116, conclusion of Question Two.

[60]Languet, p. 91, from Question Two.

ment, that is significant, and this idiom organizes the entire work.[61] Mornay never employed such an idiom; Languet regularly did.[62] Thus van Ysselsteyn's distinction between a legalist Languet and a "theological" Mornay impugns his own theory of dual authorship — a theory that is also rendered precarious by the fact that Mornay and Languet never met during the period 1574 to 1578, when the *Vindiciae* was being composed.[63] Finally, I see no reason to doubt the account in the work's Preface, which mentions only one author, who delivered to "Cono Superantius Vasco" a manuscript of *several* Questions, "prouvez et bien eclairciz."

Other kinds of internal evidence indicate Languet. His extensive experience in European diplomacy left its imprint on the *Vindiciae*. His knowledge of German affairs was well known. According to De Thou, Languet "possédait si bien les affaires d'Allemagne qu'il en instrusaient meme ceux du pays" and had given him a manuscript he had composed treating of "l'état du corps Germanique, les droits de ses diettes, le nombre et l'ordre de ses cercles," a work that was extant as late as 1745.[64] Compare the detailed description of German constitutional protocol in the *Vindiciae*.[65] Languet's expert

---

[61]Although we differ on the single author responsible, my view as to the integrity of the work is shared by Franklin:

> [van Ysselsteyn's] argument . . . is unconvincing. Almost everything depends on showing that Question 3 was once a separate treatise in view of its theme, it sources, and its style. But the style and sources follow fairly closely from the theme, so that the latter is the crucial issue. And the theme of Question 3, which deals with secular resistance, is closely related to the questions of resistance on religious grounds in Question 2. Indeed, both topics are also taken up as separate but related questions in the *Right of Magistrates*, which we know was written by one man. The organization of the *Vindiciae* is therefore natural in its time (p. 138).

On this point, cf. most recently *Vindiciae coutra tyrannos*, ed. H. Weber et al., p. iv.

[62]Cf. the few other prose works by or attributable to Languet: *Historica descriptio . . . captae urbis Gothae* (1567); the *Harangue faite au roi Charles IX* printed in the first volume of *Mémoires de l'Estat de France* (1578); the *Apologie ou Defence de tres illustre prince Guillaume* (1581) which may however be by Loyseleur de Villiers; and the *Discursus de synodo* written in 1560 and printed in the volume of letters to Augustus. Languet could have acquired this idiom, which features a sprinkling of biblical exampla over a ruthlessly legalistic exposition, from his mentor Philip Melanchthon.

[63]As was pointed out by L. Cardauns in 1903; cf. van Ysselsteyn, p. 55. Nor, apart from an unsurviving letter from Languet to Mornay of December 1574 (cf. Osborn, p. 268), do I know of any indications for correspondence between them in this period.

[64]Cf. De Thou, 11:34. Philibert Papillon noticed this manuscript in the Collection Dupuy, from which it later disappeared. Cf. Philibert Papillon, *Bibliothèque des auteurs de Bourgogne* [1745; reprinted Geneva: Slatkine Reprints, 1970], s.v. Languet.)

[65]Cf. Languet, pp. 103, 123, 130, 160–161, 166, 170, 177.

knowledge of Polish affairs is also a point to consider. We know he composed a work *De electione polonica* during the question of Henry of Anjou's election as Polish king, perhaps as a straightforward anti-Henry tract (Chevreul's conjecture), though it is reasonable to suppose that this work may also have involved some generalizations on election theory;[66] and we know that Languet's dispatches to Augustus of Saxony give careful attention to Polish affairs later in the 1570s. During the period that strikes me as the likeliest date of composition of the *Vindiciae* — from December 1575 to the summer of 1576 — Languet was providing Augustus with careful summaries of the discussions then taking place in Vienna between the Polish legates and Emperor Maximilan II concerning the Emperor's planned accession to the Polish throne. On January 29th, for example, he enclosed with his dispatch to Augustus "summam conditionum, cum quibus Imperator est electus a Polinis"; and after Maximilian took the oath to become Polish king on March 24th Languet sent a copy of "formulam Iurisandi, quod praestitit Imperator, quando Regnum Polonicum acceptavit, & scriptum, quo testatus est se Regnum acceptare iis conditionibus, de quibus inter ipsos convenit."[67] We begin to understand how the *Vindiciae* could give a circumstantial description of Polish electoral and constitutional procedure.[68] Needless to say, Mornay possessed neither the experience nor the interest in foreign constitutional questions displayed by Junius Brutus.

[4]

We may now turn to the external or anecdotal evidence (apart from Sidney's, adduced earlier) supplied by contemporaries or near-contemporaries of the French civil wars. The anecdotal evidence accuses Languet of being the sole author of the *Vindiciae* and indicates that Mornay's involvement should be limited to a small role in the preparation of Languet's text for the press in 1579, when both Languet and Mornay were associated with Orange in the Low Coun-

---

[66]For *De electione polonica*, cf. Sidney to Languet, December 19, 1573; Languet to Sidney, January 1, 1574; Sidney to Languet, January 15, 1574, as well as Chevreul, p. 210.

[67]Languet to Augustus, January 29 and March 24, 1576; cf. Mastellone, p. 400.

[68]Languet, pp. 130, 149, 151, 164, 166, 170, 177, 204.

tries. Although this material is well known, it may be helpful to go through it once again to demonstrate that it is far more homogeneous than is usually supposed. Further, it has a curious development, one that allows us to discover how and where the problem of authorship first arose. While it points to Languet as the sole author, it also tells us that Philippe de Mornay, in the last years of his life, was in the habit of telling people that the work was his own.[69]

In the first edition of his great *Histoire Universelle* (1616), Agrippa d'Aubigné wrote in one passage: "There appeared another work called Junius Brutus or a defense against tyrants, written by one of the learned gentlemen of the kingdom, reknown for several excellent books, and still living today with authority." And in another: "Hotman was long, but wrongly, suspected of writing this work, but since then a French gentleman, living as I write, has avowed to me that he was the author." Everyone agrees that this "French gentleman" was d'Aubigné's friend Mornay, who lived until 1623. However, d'Aubigné corrected both of these passages in the second edition of his work, published in 1626 after Mornay's death. To the latter passage he added: "But it has been found at last that this gentleman only *published* it, having had it in keeping from Hubert Languet." And in the former passage, he altered the word "written" to "avowed" and added: "Since then it has become known who was its real author, that is to say Hubert Languet." D'Aubigné, who was a veteran of the civil wars and a conscientious historian, seems to have taken a good deal of care to correct his first report, and to make it clear, after the death of Mornay in 1623, that Mornay had not written, but had only published, the *Vindiciae*, whose real author was Languet.[70]

The same pattern obtains in the case of Théodore Tronchin's 1628 eulogy in honor of the distinguished scholar and editor Simon Goulart. Celebrating Goulart's scholarship and general knowledge, Tronchin cited as an example his acquaintance with the history of the *Vindiciae*: "He had seen the autograph of the author, and knew that it was the work of Hubert Languet . . . which Philippe de Mornay . . . had given to the printer Thomas Guérin to be printed, and which he had published on its having come into his hands after the

---

[69]This aspect of my discussion is indebted to Barker, op cit.

[70]Aggrippa d'Aubigné, *Histoire Universelle*; 1st ed. (1616–1618), 1:91 and 2:108; 2nd ed. (1626), 1:124 and 2:670.

author's death. But [Goulart] refrained from telling the facts, in order that the ghost of so devout a man [Mornay] should not be vexed undeservedly."[71] Tronchin's testimony has sometimes been dismissed on the ground that it has one obvious inaccuracy: the *Vindiciae* was not published after Languet's death in 1581, but rather in 1579. However, another and more central aspect of his testimony has been confirmed by modern textual bibliography: Thomas Guérin of Basle was indeed the printer of the *Vindiciae*.[72] In view of this circumstantial confirmation it would be foolish to dismiss Tronchin as did, for example, Lossen.[73] His testimony yields the same pattern as that of d'Aubigné, from which it seems, *pace* Lossen, independent. We can only explain the cryptic reference to the "ghost of so devout a man being vexed" if we assume that Goulart, having heard that Mornay had claimed the *Vindiciae* as his yet knowing for a fact that he had not written the work but had only published it, "refrained from telling the facts" out of concern for Mornay's reputation; even after Mornay's death in 1623 Goulart did not wish his "ghost to be vexed undeservedly" by a charge of misrepresentation and made no public statements, as long as he lived, about the true authorship of the work. The only difference between Goulart and d'Aubigné is that d'Aubigné saw fit to set the record straight upon Mornay's death.[74]

We may discern the same pattern, of avowal from Mornay or his camp succeeded by a disinterested witness' correction, in the following items of evidence. The use of Mme de Mornay's *Mémoires* as

[71]I quote Barker's translation from Théodore Tronchin's *Oratio funebris in obitum Simonis Goulartii* (1628).

[72]See most recently Peter G. Bietenholz, *Basle and France in the Sixteenth Century: The Basle Humanists and Printers in Their Contact with Francophone Culture* (Geneva: Droz, 1971), pp. 119, 304. According to Bietenholz, the pictorial and ornamental initials used in the first edition of the *Vindiciae* "make the ascription to Guarinus virtually certain."

[73]Lossen, pp. 222-226. Characteristically, Lossen contradicts himself by substantiating the ascription to Guérin's press even while attempting to dismiss Tronchin.

[74]Cf .Barker, pp. 170-71. Although the appearance of both d'Aubigné's revised edition and Tronchin's funeral eulogy at approximately the same time (1626-1628) suggests that these testimonies may not be independent, note that each possesses a particular character: Tronchin has the fact about Guérin being the printer, whereas d'Aubigné has Mornay avowing the work (which is only implicit in Tronchin) and to him personally. Thus while d'Aubigné and Tronchin may conceivably have compared notes on the *Vindiciae* in the mid-1620s and prompted each other to a correction of the regnant theory of authorship, each made a distinctive contribution to the revised view; the overlap in their testimony suggests not that one derives from the other but that the two complement each other.

evidence has always been a favorite of Mornay partisans. In speaking of her husband's activities for the year 1574, she notes: "il fit en Latin un livre intitulé: *De la puissance légitime d'un Prince sur son peuple*, lequel a esté depuis imprimé et mis en lumière, sans toutefois que beaucoup en ayent seu l'autheur."[75] This 1574 book is generally identified with the *Vindiciae* since the title Mme de Mornay gives is strikingly similar to that of the French translation of 1581, *De la puissance légitime du Prince sur le peuple et du peuple sur le Prince* (derived from the original Latin subtitle, "De principis in populum populique in principem legitima potestate"). Yet Mme de Mornay's statement raises several objections. First, a secretary of Mornay, David de Licques, published a life of Mornay in 1647. With few exceptions this work was directly derivative of Mme de Mornay's *Mémoires*, often following the latter word for word; Licques explains that he uses the manuscript of these *Mémoires* (not published until the nineteenth century) as a constant guide, diverging only to "clarify and extend" them in the light of additional information.[76] Mornay's modern biographer thinks it significant that Licques, himself Mornay's secretary, omits the statement about the 1574 book. As Patry remarks, "L'Erreur n'est-elle pas d'avoir présenté Mornay comme l'auteur d'un ouvrage dont il n'a été que le traducteur en français et l'éditeur?"[77] The suggestion of Mornay's having been implicated only to the extent of having published or translated the *Vindiciae* is strengthened by the fact that Mme de Mornay gives not the Latin title of the work but that of the French translation.

A more serious objection to Mme de Mornay's statement is this one: the *Vindiciae* could not possibly have been composed at the time she claims, during Mornay's residence at Jametz from March to May 1574. This date is simply too early for the *Vindiciae*. First, the treatise draws heavily on Beza's *Droit des magistrats*, a work that, although written in 1573, was not circulated in manuscript and not published until *August* of 1574.[78] Second, if the passage in the *Vindiciae* about Henry of Anjou's obeying the Polish election oath is to be read ironically, as a slap at Henry for breaking that oath so spectacularly — and it seems to me that the whole force of the passage is lost if it is not so

---

[75]Mme de Mornay, *Mémoires*, 1:81.
[76]Cf. Patry, pp. 641–642.
[77]Ibid., p. 280.
[78]See Theodore Beta, *Du droit des magistrats*, ed. Robert M. Kingdon (Geneva, Droz, 1970), pp. xxx-xxxi.

read — then the composition of the *Vindiciae* must postdate Henry's notorious flight from his Polish responsibilities in *June* of 1574.[79] Third, the work recedes further from Mme de Mornay's date when we recognize its allusions to the Condé-Casimir-Anjou axis and the invasion of December 1575. Even Mornay partisans would, I think, have to agree that the spring of 1574 is too early a date for the *Vindiciae* by at least a year. Mme de Mornay's testimony is not useless, for it testifies to her husband's curious habit of avowing himself the author, but it is surely incorrect.[80]

More testimony to this habit obtains with Hugo Grotius. In a letter written in 1642, Grotius asserted that Mornay was the author of the *Vindiciae* and Orange's chaplain, Loyseleur, the publisher, adding that he derived this view principally from "the evidence of those who had lived with Mornay." A scholar named Boecler, who published a commentary on Grotius' *Law of War and Peace* in 1664, saw fit to make a detailed objection to this assertion of Mornay's authorship. In opposition to Grotius, he stated that Languet was the author. "There was a scholar at Lausanne, who possessed the manuscript written in Languet's hand, and written the way an author himself would write [ita scriptas, quasi composuerit]" — written, Barker suggests, with the erasures and corrections that betray the original author.[81]

We come now to the mainstay of the Mornay partisans — the colorful anecdote by Valentin Conrart, the seventeenth century scholar and first secretary of the French Academy. Conrart had heard from one Daillé, who had lived in Mornay's household in Saumur between 1612 and 1619, that

> in his library Mornay had a little cupboard containing only those books which he himself had written, well bound and for the most part imprinted on vellum. Among these books there was a copy of the *Junius Brutus*, which book M. Duplessis [-Mornay] had me remove any time a person of quality wished to inspect this cupboard.

[79]Cf. Languet, p. 177.

[80]It should be noted that Charlotte Arbaleste, not having shared Mornay's household until 1575, was not in a position to confirm her husband's retrospective account of prior years. One doubts she should be held responsible for the inaccuracy.

[81]Cf. Barker, p. 171. The original, which I quote after Lossen, reads: "Mihi videtur auctorem fuisse Hub. Languetum:-Losannae fuit vir doctus, qui pagellas habuit scriptas manu ipsius Langueti, et quidem ita scriptas, quasi composuerit; deinde stylus cum ipsius stylo congruit."

He would give me the key and tell me to run ahead and open the
door, adding in a low voice or otherwise indicating that I should
remove this book of *Junius Brutus* from view; for M. Duplessis was
well aware that this book had not the approval of everyone, and
wished to avoid discussing it.

It is not clear that this anecdote constitutes proof of Mornay's authorship of the *Vindiciae*. What it tells us is what we have already
learned from d'Aubigné, Goulart, Grotius, and Mme de Mornay—
that Mornay was, or wished his circle to think he was, in some way
connected with the *Vindiciae*. It is not inconsistent with the considered view of d'Aubigné and Goulart that Mornay's role was limited
to seeing the book through the press. Nor is it inconsistent with the
suggestion, derived in connection with Mme de Mornay's *Mémoires*,
that Mornay executed the French translation. This is the view of the
matter taken by Barker as well as by Patry, who adds that at the time
of Daillé's service in Mornay's household, Mornay was urging the
submission of Protestants to the crown and may have judged it prudent not to display for visitors a book that sanctioned rebellion.[82]

This external or anecdotal evidence can obviously be construed in
different ways. At the end of the nineteenth century Mornay's partisans made much of the Conrart anecdote and tried to lessen the
impact of d'Aubigné and Tronchin by suggesting that Mornay's avowal of authorship must count for more than their explicit corrections. This was a doubtful procedure since they had simultaneously
to endorse one aspect of d'Aubigné and Tronchin (the main witnesses for Mornay's avowal) while discounting another (the same witnesses' considered rejection of Mornay in favor of Languet). It
seems to me that we should either accept these witnesses entirely,
including their testimony for Languet, or discount them entirely. In
fact, the evidence of all the witnesses falls into a coherent pattern —
of avowal of authorship from Mornay's camp followed by sub-

---

[82]Barker, pp. 169–170; Patry, pp. 280–281. For the original, cf. Valentin Conrart,
Mémoires sur l'histoire de son temps; in *Mémoires relatifs a l'histoire de France*, ed. Petitot
(Paris, 1838), p. 622. Curiously, the same Daillé who was Conrart's source for this
anecdote seems to have told another man of letters "qu'il avait appris que l'auteur du
livre intitulé *Vindiciae contra Tyrannos*, sous le nom de Stéphanus Junius Brutus, est
Hubert Languet, savant homme et grand politique" (cf. Bayle, p. 126, quoting Colomiès' *Opuscules* [1669]). While the chronological relation of Daillé's two testimonies is
not clear to me, and while that in favor of Languet may simply reflect awareness of
d'Aubigné's revisions, it may be that Daillé fits our pattern whereby evidence for
Mornay prompts correction in favor of Languet.

sequent correction (if I may include Licques' silently editing Mme de
Mornay as a correction) by fairly disinterested witnesses, none of
whom can be said to have had any personal interest in championing
Languet (the opposite is true if anything: d'Aubigné knew and re-
spected Mornay, and Licques had been his secretary and biographer; they were simply concerned to set the record straight).
Three of the corrections are fairly circumstantial. Two of them
(those of Goulart and Boecler) indicate an autograph of the *Vindiciae*
in Languet's hand; two of them (Goulart and d'Aubigné) carefully
restrict Mornay to the role of publisher; one of them (that of
Goulart) contains a fact that has been verified independently (that
Guérin of Basle was the printer). Given the unambiguous verdict of
internal evidence as well as the care with which Mornay is corrected
on this issue by impartial contemporaries, I don't see that we have
any choice but to accept Barker's conclusion—that in the last few
years of his life Mornay was in the habit of exaggerating any share
he may have had in the production of the *Vindiciae*. "He did not
indeed make any explicit claim to its authorship (the *Vindiciae* was
not a book to be avowed openly), but he let it be understood—
mysteriously and yet suggestively—that he knew, that he was concerned, that he had published, in a word, that it was his. This involves, of course, a serious charge of wholesale plagiarism—the
plagiarism, in fact, of a whole book. It is a charge that can only be
made with reluctance; but if we come to the conclusion that the
balance of external evidence is in favor of Languet, it is a charge
which cannot be avoided."[83]

I pointed earlier to a fundamental inconsistency between Mornay's lifelong stance as an irenic Politique royalist and the purposes
of the *Vindiciae*. How then begin to explain his avowal of the work
late in life (for the reports suggest that this did not begin until a
decade or so into the seventeenth century)? The very insistence and
selflessness of his devotion to the Politique perspective may
paradoxically provide an answer. Mornay spent thirty-four years
furthering the purposes of that great monarch who embodied the
Politique attitude—Henry IV. For his service he did not receive
commensurate reward. Though one of Henry's chief counsellors in
the years before the accession and one of his staunchest defenders in

---

[83]Barker, p. 173. Barker indicates another occasion on which the older Mornay
apparently made free with factual materials in order to suit his own purposes.

the difficult decade of the 1590s, Mornay was rewarded with nothing more than a provincial governorship. By the turn of the century he found himself eclipsed from the king's view by the duc de Sully, who went on to become Henry IV's most influential adviser. For the "pape des Huguenots" this was a bitter pill. Indeed we can gather from Mme de Mornay that it was the central tragedy of his life. No one had defended the throne more sedulously; no one in Henry's original circle now seemed further from it. Not that Mornay abdicated now from his lifelong royalism — even from Saumur he continued to defend Paris against the provinces — but it should not surprise us were he to begin regarding his peripheral involvement, some three decades earlier, in a cause diametrically opposed to his regular one with a certain nostalgia, and even (given the crown's continued inability to reward his faith as well as the absence of knowledgeable witnesses) to magnify that involvement. Thanks to his disappointment, he reached ever so tentatively through to the position that it had been his lifelong practice to reject.[84]

[5]

There need never have arisen the "problem" of the *Vindiciae*. The problem arose only because we mistrusted the evidence, which in fact displays a coherent pattern. The argument in which, late in his life, Mornay sought obliquely to participate, no one in 1576 had denounced with greater eloquence than he himself, when he warned the French that self-appointed political messiahs were apt to do far more harm than Henry III ("Il s'en levera quelqu'ung qui se dira protecteur de la liberté, qui accablera le peuple de plus dure

---

[84]As for the Conrart anecdote, a friend with a psychoanalytic bent puts an interesting construction on Mornay's behavior. In order to "avoid discussing" the *Vindiciae*, Mornay had his servant remove it from the cabinet displaying his own works whenever a visitor wished to inspect it, not so much because it defended a controversial thesis as because he knew it had no place in that cabinet — for unlike the other works there, it simply wasn't his. This strikes me as a more comprehensive explanation of the anecdote (the truth of which I see no need to deny) than that of Patry or Barker. Mornay could participate in the aura of this increasingly notorious work by allowing it to sit there *en famille*, and could let others obliquely understand that he'd somehow been in on it (a marginally justifiable claim); but he was unable to progress from this kind of behavior to such a public, systematic claim as would be indicated by allowing visitors to view the book within the cabinet of his own works.

servitude qu'il ne porte").[85] Putting aside his late, unhappy flirtation (was he specifically repenting it in the codicil to his will, when he admonished his inheritors never to be tempted by the spirit of insurrection?), Mornay's views and career amount to something very nearly the opposite of Languet's. One took the path of irenicism and followed — perhaps too selflessly — Henry IV; the other took the path of godly opposition and readily served those great lords (e.g., John Casimir and Anjou) whom — perhaps naively — he appointed instruments of a Calvinist theocracy. For all but those who insist on seeing answers face to face, the question as to which of these two men wrote the *Vindiciae contra tyrannos* need detain us no longer.

[85]From the 1576 *Remonstrance aux etats de Blois*; in Mornay, *Mémoires et correspondance*, 2:74. Mornay may be thinking partly of François d'Anjou, who months earlier had in effect styled himself "protecteur de la liberté" in the justificatory *Protestation* (s.l., 1575) he published on the eve of his revolt.

APPENDIX B

Fulke Greville on "Ister Banke"

THE NAME OF FULKE GREVILLE (1554–1628), Sidney's friend and biographer and a considerable poet in his own right, intersects the story of Philisides' beast-fable not once or twice but four different times. Greville was directly responsible for the appearance of "Ister banke" in print; he drew on the fable in a work of his own; he alluded to this text in his seventeenth century biography of Sidney; and finally he is mentioned in it. Following out each of these connections helps to throw light on Sidney's text.

1) Greville is mentioned in the text. I am referring to an allusion in the frame stanzas, 11. 39–40:

> Till [Languet and I were] forste to parte, with harte and eyes even
> sore,
> To worthy Coredens he gave me ore.

Coredens, a variation on the Virgilian shepherd Corydon, evidently refers to a historical figure to whom Hubert Languet once entrusted the young Sidney. Coredens is also mentioned in the Third and Fourth Eclogues of *Old Arcadia* as a shepherd friend of Philisides who like him is hopelessly in love with Mira (4:229, 318). This suggests Coredens is Fulke Greville since Mira is one of the ladies — whether fictional or real is irrelevant — whom Greville addresses in his lyric sequence *Caelica* (cf., e.g., poems 7, 14–15, 22–25, 27–35). Greville calls himself "Myraphill" (lover of Myra) in *Caelica* 73; and one of the contributors to the Oxford *Exequiae* (1586) on Sidney used

143

the code name "Miraphilus" for Greville.[1] Coredens' amorous competition with Philisides for Mira's favors may reflect the fact that some of Greville's early love lyrics in the *Caelica* sequence, which he said were "Written in his Youth, and familiar Exercise with Sir Philip Sidney," counterpoint a number of Sidney's lyrics in the *Astrophil and Stella* sequence.[2]

The identification of Coredens with Greville explains Languet's "giving over" of Sidney to Coredens. Languet met Greville when he accompanied Sidney on the embassy to the German princes in 1577. Sidney, Greville, and Languet spent several weeks together on the trip through the German states before the two Englishmen parted with Languet at Cologne in May to return to England, at which time Languet "gave [Sidney] ore" to Greville.[3] In the first letter Languet wrote to Sidney after the latter's return to England, he asked to be remembered to the generous Mr. Greville, who was Sidney's "necessarium" or indispensable friend.[4] Ringler's suggestion that "Coredens" is a made-up compound "Co-red[i]ens" meaning "returning with" may thus not be far-fetched, for it tallies with Greville's 1577 return voyage with Sidney.[5]

Although I cautioned earlier against expending too much energy on finding extra-fictional references behind the frame stanzas (simply because the fable itself should be our primary concern), it should be noted that a spring 1577 date for the discussions of Languet and Sidney to which the fable refers correlates with everything else we have learned. This was the moment that saw Languet, his plans for publishing the *Vindiciae* temporarily frustrated, share at some length with Sidney his ideas, surely including his political program if not the manuscript itself ("I felt incredible satisfaction from our intercourse during so many days").[6] One may assume that Sidney's

---

[1] See Geoffrey Bullough (ed.), *The Poems and Dramas of Fulke Greville* (New York: Oxford University Press, 1945) 1:40–41.

[2] For correspondences between Greville's lyrics and Sidney's, cf. M. W. Croll, *The Works of Fulke Greville: A Thesis* (Philadelphia: J. B. Lippincott, 1903), pp. 8–11; Bullough's annotations passim; and Joan Rees, *Fulke Greville, Lord Brooke* (Berkeley: University of California Press, 1971), pp. 87–103.

[3] On the 1577 embassy, cf. James Osborn, *Young Philip Sidney* (New Haven: Yale University Press, 1972), pp. 480–493.

[4] Languet to Sidney, June 14, 1577.

[5] William A. Ringler (ed.), *The Poems of Sir Philip Sidney* (Oxford: Clarendon Press, 1962), p. 413; but he puts the etymological analysis in the service of another candidate for Coredens.

[6] Languet to Sidney, June 14, 1577, trans. Pears. His letter to Augustus of June 8 contains an extended *elogium* of Sidney.

"necessarium," who later remembered Languet as an "excellent teacher," "learned *usque ad miraculum*," took some part in these discussions.[7]

2) Greville was directly responsible for the appearance in print of "Ister banke." Sidney left the unfinished revision of his epic, or what we now know as the *New Arcadia*, in the care of Greville when he went to the Low Countries in November 1585. Never having revised the original Eclogue material, Sidney left the decision for arranging this material in the new version to Greville, as Greville explained when he printed the fragmentary *New Arcadia* in 1590: "If any defect be found in the Eclogues, which although they were of Sir Phillip Sidneis writing, yet were they not perused by him, but left till the worke had been finished, that then choise should have bene made, which should have been taken, and in what manner brought in. At this time they have bene chosen and disposed as the over-seer thought best" (1:4).[8]

Greville "thought best" to relocate a number of poems from the later Eclogues of the original *Arcadia* in order that these poems be printed in 1590, and one of these was Philisides' beast-fable. For since the 1590 text breaks off in the middle of the Third Book, it does not reach as far as the Third Eclogues, where the fable originally appeared, and thus the fable would not have been printed in 1590 had not Greville chosen to transpose it to an earlier Eclogue, namely the First. As "over-seer," Greville also shifted two poems of Strephon and Klaius, originally in the Fourth Eclogues, putting one in each of the first two Eclogues; shifted the discussion of marriage between Geron and Histor from Third to First; and, to make room for the additions to the early Eclogues, omitted two poems in classical scansion from the First and three such poems from the Second. The part of Philisides was also reduced. Sidney himself in the revised *Arcadia* had already redistributed among other characters a number of songs that had originally belonged to Philisides, and it was perhaps by way of complying with his intention to reduce Philisides' part that Greville proceeded to remove Philisides from the Eclogues. Thus it is not Philisides but a nameless "yong shepherd" who sings "Ister banke" in the *New Arcadia*.

Greville's taking special care to relocate "Ister banke" so that it

---

[7] Fulke Greville, *Life of Sir Philip Sidney* (Oxford: Clarendon Press, 1907), pp. 7–8.
[8] For Greville's editing the *New Arcadia* with Matthew Gwynne, cf. Ringler, p. 370. I think it is safe to say that of the two, Greville made the important editorial decisions.

might be printed indicates a proprietary interest on his part in this particular text. It seems reasonable to suppose that this interest has something to do with Greville's own part, as Sidney's "necessarium," in the discussion to which the introductory stanzas refer—a part that Sidney himself had acknowledged by mentioning "worthy Coredens."

3) Greville drew on the fable in a work of his own. Perhaps late in the 1590s, in any event years after Sidney's death, Greville composed a *Treatise of Monarchy*. In one section of this fiercely royalist work, a section advising "weake minded tyrants" on how to maintain order, Greville gives a capsule version of our fable:

> For as when birdes and beasts would have a kinge,
> To furnish this faire creature for a guide,
> Out of their owne they gave him everie thinge,
> And by their guifts themselves more surely tyde;
>   Eyes, voyces, winges, and of their natures skill,
>   To governe, rayse, or ruyne them at will:
>
> Soe may these fraile unactive kinde of spiritts
> [i.e., the "weake minded tyrants"]
> Be with the milke of many nurses fedd,
> All strivinge to hold upp the scepter rights
> With subjects strength by Crownes authorised;
>   Whereby the feeble may againe be wombed,
>   And there gett life, even where it was intombed.[9]

Greville's modern editor notes: "I have not been able to trace this fable."[10] Greville found this fable nowhere else but in Sidney's "Ister banke," which he himself had been responsible for printing in 1590. The point is not so much that Greville recalls Philisides' fable as that his view of the fable confirms our reading of it. Greville gets right to the point: the community of animals now quite explicitly alienates all of its rights or "guifts" to the crown ("To governe, rayse, or ruyne them at will"). Just as Man, intrinsically a weaker force, utilizes attributes that were once the beasts' in order to subdue them to his purpose ("And by their guifts themselves more surely tyde"), so even a feeble monarch may draw strength from the collective sac-

---

[9] Fulke Greville, *Treatise of Monarchy*, stt. 122–23; in *Remains: Being Poems of Monarchy and Religion*, ed. G. A. Wilkes (Oxford: University Press, 1965), pp. 65–66.
[10] G. A. Wilkes in *Remains*, p. 238.

rifice of subjects' rights — "Be with the milke of many nurses fedd,/ All stringe to hold upp the scepter rights." Thus Greville's reading of the fable confirms the view elaborated in the present study, according to which Sidney views the bestial donation of rights to Man as irreversibly binding. Significantly, Greville also develops the absolutist view of the *pactum subjectionis* in an earlier stanza of his treatise concerning that scriptural episode which served as Sidney's model — Israel's wilful transition to monarchy. The poet is cautioning the community not to begrudge tyranny:

> Man then repyne not at these boundless kinges,
> Since yow endure the fate of your forefathers,
> To whom God did foretell, on humane winges
> How inequality once rais'd, still gathers;
>   Their choice offended him, please you it must,
>   Whose dreggs still in you, on you make it just.[11]

Greville's syntax, characteristically more elliptical than Sidney's, calls for some analysis. The third and fourth lines of the stanza refer to God's warning to Israel through Samuel (1 Samuel 8), construing this passage in the absolutist manner: the forefathers' original election or "raising" of a king above the rest of the community created an "inequality" that succeeding generations would ineluctably inherit ("How inequality once rais'd, still [forever] gathers"). From this act, which constitutes at once the community's apostasy from God and its requisite punishment, there is presently no escape or appeal ("Their choice offended him [i.e., God], please you it must"). The "dreggs" of the sixth line are those of the original choice for a king, so called by analogy with those of Adam's original disobedience; entailed to every generation, the presence of this inherited sin *within* you justifies the monarch's vigilant dominion *over* you ("Whose dreggs still *in* you, *on* you make it just" [my emphasis]). Note that the present stanza contains a reminiscence of the beast fable fashioned after this scriptural episode of which Greville provides an epitome elsewhere in his *Treatise*: "God did foretell, *on humane winges*/ How inequality once rais'd . . . [my emphasis]" Monarchy's appearance "on humane winges," meaningless apart from the context of Philisides' beast fable, conflates Sidney's progressivist "after" ("humane") with his bestial "before" ("winges") into

---

[11]Greville, *Treatise of Monarchy*, st. 25, p. 41.

an oxymoron. This and Greville's later reference in stanza 122 ("eyes, voyces, *winges*") hark back to 11. 99–101 of Philisides' fable:

> Each other beast likewise his present brings:
> And (but they drad their Prince they ofte should want)
> They all consented were to give him wings:

Greville's regular position throughout the *Treatise of Monarchy* is that the community's original freedom is no longer available. Like Sidney, he censures the libertarian attempt to return sovereignty "to that whence it began" (st. 26), that is, to the community.

Indeed, much in Greville's *Treatise* apart from these specific reminiscences is relevant to Sidney's politics. The subtitles of some individual sections — "The Excellencie of Monarchy Compared with Aristocratie"; "The Excellencie of Monarchy Compared with Democratie"; "The Excellencie of Monarchy Compared with Aristocratie and Democratie Joyntly" — echo themes that have recurred throughout this study. The *Treatise of Monarchy* is one long paean to the Bodinian conception of the state and of sovereignty.[12] Greville differs from Sidney principally in not allowing the libertarian position much of a hearing, although it is true that a character in the first version of his closet drama *Mustapha* trots out the argument for just rebellion.[13] Greville's epitome of Philisides' beast fable indicates that he was privy to the real meaning of Sidney's text, its witty progressivist tilt as against its ostensible primitivism.

4) Greville alluded to "Ister banke" in his biography of Sidney, written between 1610–1612. In the course of his praise of Languet, whom he remembered as an "excellent teacher," "learned *usque ad miraculum*; wise by the conjunction of practice in the world with the well-grounded theory of books," he noted that Languet had been "mentioned for honours sake in Sir Philips *Arcadia*."[14] This can only refer to the "Ister banke" eclogue since Languet is mentioned nowhere else in Sidney's work. Greville's recollection of this particular text more than twenty years after it had appeared in print should not surprise us in view of what we have learned about his interest in

---

[12]Cf. Hugh McLean, "Fulke Greville: Kingship and Sovereignty," *Huntington Library Quarterly* 16 (1952–53), 237–271.

[13]Even within the play, however, Achmat eventually rejects this position. Cf. Fulke Greville, *Poems and Dramas* 2:34–38.

[14]Greville, *Life of Sidney*, p. 8.

its genesis, publication, and theme. His statement that Sidney had mentioned Languet "for honours sake" need not contradict the view of this study. Although Greville evidently perceived that "Ister banke" fashioned a criticism of "old Languet" — this much should be evident from the nature of his epitome in the *Treatise of Monarchy* — he knew that it was nonetheless grounded in personal involvement and concern since he himself combined fairly unqualified rejection of Languet's monarchomach politics with the warmest regard for his person. Thus it was possible for Sidney to mention Languet "for honours sake" even while developing a critique of his ideas. Indeed Sidney allowed the name of no other contemporary to appear in his fiction. Thanks to him, Hubert Languet's memory would not "die from the earth for want of an epitaph."

Index

Addleshaw, Percy, 11
Aeschylus, 81
Airo-Farulla, Joseph A., 129n
Albada, Aggaeus, 122
Allen, J. W., 28
Amadis de Gaule, 36–37
d'Anjou, François duc d'Alençon et, 20,
  26–33, 36–38, 60, 72, 100n, 104,
  115–117, 120–126, 127n, 137, 141
Arendt, Hannah, 103, 106, 108
Aristotle, 6, 24, 40, 50, 51, 81, 82, 104,
  131
Athens, 39–40
D'Aubigné, Agrippa, 120n, 134, 138–
  139
Augustus, Elector of Saxony, 116–119,
  121, 133

Bancroft, Richard, 105n
Barclay, William, 3, 42, 73n, 75n
Barker, Arthur, 113n, 114, 127n, 134n,
  137, 138, 139
Bayle, Pierre, 113n, 128, 138n
Becker, Carl, 5
Belleforest, François, 73n
Belloy, Pierre de, 126n
Benert, Richard R., 23n
Bergbusch, Martin, 19n, 48–49, 51n,
  65n, 69n, 104n
Berson, Jacques, 31n

Beza, Theodore, 10, 65n, 103; *Du droit
  des magistrats* 4, 5–6, 12, 22n, 26,
  41–42, 56n, 72, 76n, 103, 127, 131,
  132n, 136
Bietenholz, Peter G., 135n
Bill, Alfred H., 59n
Blackwood, Adam, 42, 75n, 123
Bodin, Jean, 89, 148; *La République* 43,
  54–56, 73n, 104, 105n
Boecler, J. H., 137, 139
Bradley, W. A., 59n
Briggs, W. D., 19n, 22, 48–49, 65n,
  104n
Buchanan, George, 9, 65n, 71n, 103,
  114; *De jure regni apud Scotos* 4, 6, 65,
  130
Bullough, Geoffrey, 144n

Calvin, John, 24, 42, 75, 76
Camerarius, Joachim I and II, 120n,
  121n
Casimir, John, Count Palatine, 26, 33,
  115–116, 123, 126, 137, 141
Cervantes, Miguel de, 35
Charles IX, 4, 8
Chevreul, Henri, 35n, 100n, 122n, 133n
Church, W. F., 107n
Cicero, 40, 133
Coke, Sir Edward, 105n
Coleridge, S. T., 130

Coligny, Gaspard de, 8
Coligny, Louise de, 9
Collins, Arthur, 104n
Colomiès, Paul, 138n
Condé, Henri I, duc de, 8
Condé, Henri II, duc de, 26, 33, 124n,
    126, 137
Connell, Dorothy, 104n
Conrart, Valentin, 137–138, 140
Contarini, Gasparo, 40, 41, 53–54
Croll, M. W., 144n
Cromwell, Thomas, 42

Daillé, 137, 138n
Dale, Valentine, 105n
Davis, Sarah M., 59n
De Crue de Stoutz, Francis, 27n, 127n
Denkinger, E. M., 59n
Diderot, Denis, 19
Diodorus Siculus, 49n
Drake, Sir Francis, 103
Droz, E., 26n
Dryden, John, 57
Dudley, Mary, 7
Dyer, Edward, 11n, 55n

Elizabeth I, 7–8, 27, 30, 108n, 109, 121
Elkan, A., 113n, 127–128
Estienne, Henri, 9, 10, 37, 93, 118–119,
    122

Fauchet, Claude, 73n
Fay, Michel Hurault, seigneur du, 126n
Figgis, J. N., 126n
Fink, Zera, 42
Fogel, Ephim, 11n, 65n, 99n, 100n
Foote, D. N., x
Fox Bourne, H. R., 59n
Franklin, J. H., 4n, 131n, 132n
Freegard, William, 130n

Gentillet, Innocent, 27n, 32n, 75n
Giannotti, Donato, 41, 53–54
Giesey, Ralph, 4n
Gilbert, Allan, 55n
Godshalk, William, ix
Golding, Arthur, 9
Goldman, Marcus, 49, 55n, 59n
Gorboduc, 12

Goulart, Simon, 134–135, 138, 139
Greenlaw, Edwin, 27
Grégoire, Pierre, 126n
Greville, Fulke, 25, 39, 55, 75n, 143–
    149
Griffiths, Gordon, 123n
Grotius, Hugo, 73n, 75n, 105, 121n,
    137, 138
Guérin, Thomas, 134–135, 139
Guicciardini, Francesco, 40

Haag, Eugene and Emile, 100n, 117n
Harrington, James, 41
Harvey, Gabriel, 3
Hauser, Henri, 127
Henry II, 36
Henry III, 4, 26, 27, 29, 31, 33, 115,
    120, 122, 125, 128n, 133, 136–137, 139
Henry IV (Henry of Navarre), 8, 20,
    125, 128–129, 139–141
Herodotus, 104
Homer, 79
Hooker, Richard, 12, 73n, 104, 105, 108
l'Hôpital, Michel de, 126
Hotman, François, 3, 8–9, 20, 37, 65n,
    103, 134; Francogallia 4, 5–6, 20, 71,
    72
Hotman, Jean, 10
Howell, Roger, 59n

Jagger, Graham, 129–130

Kelley, Donald M., 103n
Kervyn de Lettenhove, Joseph, baron,
    29n, 122n

Languet, Hubert, 3, 6–7, 9–11, 12–17,
    20, 30–31, 37–38, 53, 58–61, 65, 67,
    70, 71, 72, 76, 77, 86–87, 89, 93–94,
    98n, 99–100, 103–104, 113–141 pas-
    sim, 143–145, 148–149; see also Vin-
    diciae contra tyrannos
La Noue, François de, 36–37, 126n
Leicester, Robert Dudley, Earl of, 7–9
Levine, Norman, 65n, 89n
Levy, C. S., 65n
Licques, David de, 136, 139
Lingelsheim, Michael, 10, 93
Locke, John, 11

Lossen, Max, 113n, 122n, 129n, 130, 135
Louis XI, 42
Lycurgus, 41

McCoy, Richard, 19–20, 34
Machiavelli, Niccolo, 40, 41, 117, 118n, 119
MacLean, Hugh, 55n, 148n
Marnix, Philippe de, 37, 71n, 122–123
Marsilius of Padua, 4
Mastellone, Salvo, 28n, 33n, 113n, 115, 123
Maximilian II, 115, 118n, 133
de'Medici, Catherine, 4, 8, 27, 120
Melanchthon, Philip, 9, 132n
Milton, John, 41
Molyneaux, Edmund, 58
Montaigne, Michel de, 129
Montgomery, Gabriel, count, 36
Mornay, Mme de (Charlotte Arbaleste), 135–140
Mornay, Philippe de, sieur de Plessis-Marly, 3, 9, 30, 113–114, 123n, 124–141
Motley, J. L., x
Myrick, Kenneth, 37n

Nepos, Cornelius, 42n
Nevers, Louis de Gonzague, duc de, 8, 120n
Nimrod, 70

Oliva, P., 55n
Orange, William of, x, 9, 10, 30, 37, 60, 104, 116, 121, 122n, 123, 124n, 133, 137
Osborn, James, 8, 30n, 92n, 117n, 118n, 144n
Ovid, 64, 70, 80, 82
Oxford, Earl of, 108n

Panofsky, Erwin, 86n
Papillon, Philibert, 132n
Paruta, Paolo, 41
Pasquier, Etienne, 126
Patry, Raoul, 127, 128
Pausanias, 49n
Philip II, 10, 123
Pibrac, Guy du Faur, sieur de, 126n

Piero di Cosimo, 85–86
Plato, 41, 50, 130
Plotinus, 130
Plutarch, 41, 49, 50–51
Polybius, 16, 40, 41
Ponet, John, 41
Prometheus, 65, 84
Pufendorf, Samuel, 52n, 73n
Pythagoras, 80, 82

Raleigh, Sir Walter, 105n
Rawson, Elizabeth, 43n, 51n
Rees, Joan, 144n
Renouard, A. A., 118n
Reveille-Matin, 6, 71
Reynolds, Beatrice, 30n
Ribner, Irving, 19, 49, 65n, 69
Richter, B. L. O., 125n, 128n
Ringler, William A., Jr., 46, 59n, 65n, 67, 69, 94n, 98n, 144n
Robertson, Jean, 58, 59n, 65n, 94n, 98n, 105
Rogers, Daniel, 10
Rousseau, Jean-Jacques, 16, 41

Salmon, J. H. M., 3
Sargent, R. M., 55n
Seneca, 130
Shakespeare, William, 12, 62n, 104
Sidney, Sir Henry, 7, 104n
Sidney, Mary, Countess of Pembroke, 46
Sidney, Sir Philip
  —Life: 7–11, 29–30
  —Works:
    Apology for Poetry, 16, 17, 38, 85n, 89, 99–100, 110
    Arcadia (both versions), 7, 11–17
      Old Arcadia, 20, 39–40, 57–77, 79–101, 106–107, 110, 143–149
      New Arcadia, 8, 19–38, 40, 43–56, 88, 104, 107–108, 145
    Astrophil and Stella, 14, 38, 89, 93, 110
Sidney, Robert, 53, 58, 104
Sinfield, Alan, 93n
Smith, Sir Thomas, 105
Sophocles, 81

Sparta (Laconia, Lacedemonia), 15,
    39–56, 107
Spenser, Edmund, 58
Sully, Maximilien de Béthune, duc
    de, 140
Sydney, Algernon, 41
Symonds, J. A., 59n

Talbert, E. W., 59n
Thoré, duc de, 126
Thucydides, 49n, 50
Tronchin, Theodore, 134–135

Ursinus, Zacharias, 117n

Valois, Margaret of, 8
van Dorsten, J. A., 10n, 65n, 94n,
    100n
van Ysselsteyn, G. T., 131–132
Venice, 53–55
Villiers, Loyseleur de, 60, 121,
    132n, 137

Vindiciae contra tyrannos, xi, 4, 5–7,
    9, 10, 12, 20, 22n, 23, 26–27,
    30–33, 37, 41–42, 56n, 57–59,
    65–70, 72, 76, 93–94, 100, 108,
    113–141 passim; see also Lan-
    guet, Hubert
Virgil, 97
Visser, Derek, 113n

Waddington, A., 113n
Walker, D. P., 128n
Walsingham, Sir Francis, 7, 10
Walzer, Michael, 24, 34–35, 36, 71
Weber, Henri, 113n, 132n
Weill, G., 73n
Wilkes, G. A., 146n
Wills, Gary, 5

Xenophon, 49n

Zampini, Matteo, 73n
Zouch, Thomas, 7, 59n